ISBN 978-0-243-08959-8
PIBN 10774350

1 MONTH OF
FREE
READING

at

www.ForgottenBooks.com

By purchasing this book you are eligible for one month membership to ForgottenBooks.com, giving you unlimited access to our entire collection of over 1,000,000 titles via our web site and mobile apps.

To claim your free month visit:

www.forgottenbooks.com/free774350

English
Français
Deutsche
Italiano
Español
Português

www.forgottenbooks.com

Mythology Photography **Fiction**
Fishing Christianity **Art** Cooking
Essays Buddhism Freemasonry
Medicine **Biology** Music **Ancient
Egypt** Evolution Carpentry Physics
Dance Geology **Mathematics** Fitness
Shakespeare **Folklore** Yoga Marketing
Confidence Immortality Biographies
Poetry **Psychology** Witchcraft
Electronics Chemistry History **Law**
Accounting **Philosophy** Anthropology
Alchemy Drama Quantum Mechanics
Atheism Sexual Health **Ancient History**
Entrepreneurship Languages Sport
Paleontology Needlework Islam
Metaphysics Investment Archaeology
Parenting Statistics Criminology
Motivational

CONTENTS

Introduction

General Descripton of Prof. Livingstone's French Dresscutting Machine

Equipment required

 ©CIA683232

Costume Designing
Pattern Drafting
Dresscutting

INTRODUCTION

This course contains a series of instructions on the use and application of Prof. J. W. Livingstone's FRENCH DRESSCUTTING MACHINE, Patented in 1905, improved 1915, 1921, for the designing and cutting of women's and children's garments.

It is intended that with these instructions anyone who can read and understand the English language, can take Prof. Livingstone's FRENCH DRESSCUTTING MACHINE and with it. design any garment of every style and make practical working patterns to fit any woman's figure.

ACCURACY, Importance of

The student upon taking up the study of this work should at once learn the importance of accuracy, carefulness, and thoroughness. As early as possible the student should form the habit of making a mind's picture of the garment she intends to design. This does not mean, however, that there will not be changes in ideas as first conceived; to the contrary, seldom is a design ever completed as it was originally planned.

READ ENTIRE LESSON

These instructions are divided into short, accurately worded lessons and the student should master each one thoroughly as they occur before proceeding to the next, and read the entire lesson over several times before starting to execute the design.

ATTENTION

A very important point on the study from text is to give the entire mind and thought over to the subject, and never pass a paragraph or even a sentence until it is thoroughly impressed upon the mind.

A great many people have the habit of reading one subject and thinking along another line altogether. One cannot study successfully in this way. The text must have your entire mind.

SUCCESS MEANS STUDY

Determination must be the watch-word. Anything that is worth while may seem impossible at first when after a short time of honest study, it will clarify itself in your mind to where you wonder why you did not understand it at first glance.

ANY CHANGE OF STYLE

Prof. Livingstone's FRENCH DRESSCUTTING MACHINE is so designed that no matter what the change of fashion might be, it can readily be adapted thereto.

You learn to make the foundations first.

DESIGN AND CUTTING MOST IMPORTANT

While the knowledge of making seams and stitches is a very important requisite in costume building, it is of secondary importance to the beginner in the study of these Arts.

ATTENTION TO PLATES AND TEXT

It is very important that the student pay strict attention to both the written text and the illustrated plates. One must have the ambition to master the points that are apparently most difficult and very careful to understand the intent of the text, and doubly careful in executing the instruction correctly. Do not try to get ahead of the text. Read each sentence then carry out instruction given by it before proceeding to the next.

General Description of
PROF. LIVINGSTONE'S FRENCH DRESSCUTTING MACHINE

To get the best results from any machine or mechanical appliance, the user must be thoroughly familiar with all of its parts. With that purpose in view. this chapter is written.

ADJUSTABLE PATTERN

The machine is an adjustable pattern, adaptable to all shapes and sizes of women's figures. It is composed of two major parts, the waist or above the belt, and the skirt, or below the belt.

ONE HALF OF DESIGN

It is customary in the making of patterns *to make only one-half of a design,* that is when the design is identical on both sides of the center back or center front. Therefore, we first learn to draft plain patterns for one-half of the garment working from center front around the left side to center back.

FAMILIARIZE YOURSELF WITH MACHINE

You should first of all arrange your machine out in front of you on a board or table and read over carefully every word on each section. The arrangement should be made as shown on Plate 1, which is the large plate in the center of the book.

BASQUE OR UPPER GARMENT SECTION

The waist or basque is composed of eight component parts, viz., front section A-C, double under-arm D-D, single under-arm S-B, side back A-D, center back L-L; two sections for the sleeves; T-S, U-S, together with the designing scale or rule, which is graduated from one to eighteen inches for the making of measurements, reproducing illustrations. and producing irregular curves at required locations as you will learn later. Each movable part has a reference number with which to identify it.

The upper or waist machine is made to reproduce a perfect tight-fitting English basque or two dart fitted lining with four seams on either side and sometimes at the center back. (See Plate 1.)

FOUNDATION FOR GARMENTS

This design is and always will be the foundation for all fitted garments and from it the user soon learns to design any garment that may come in style from time to time.

EASILY ADAPTED

It is very easily adapted to the Princess or Empire styles (See Glossary for definition of these words), French linings, and the loose fancy frocks, blouses and kimona foundations; giving also the correct foundation for all tailored garments, both plain and fancy.

NO REFITTING

Properly and carefully used it eliminates all refitting because it is set to the required sizes to begin with, thereby, appreciably reducing the time and labor usually required in correct garment making.

DESCRIPTION OF SKIRT SECTION

The skirt section consists of a rigid segment which has a graduated measure to give the size and proper curve for the waist and hip lines. There are two adjustable sliding scales with measures thereon to give the desired lengths and shape of the skirt. It is designed to cut a plain two-piece, gored or circular skirt, to all sizes. These being the foundation for all modern skirts. The fancy and novelty skirts are developed from the above foundations. See Plate 10.

PATTERNS, The Need of

Anyone, before they can advance very far in the Art of costume designing, must learn to make working patterns for the design required to fit the individual for whom the garment is to be made.

A knowledge of pattern making is therefore required to be able to draw the model or guide which when completed and cut out, makes the pattern.

EQUIPMENT AND SUPPLIES REQUIRED

Prof. Livingstone's French Dresscutting Machine.
A table or board. Size about three feet square or larger.
Paper for drafting. Plain Manila or white. Size 20 by 30 inches or larger.
Lead pencil (soft).
Cloth tape measure (60 inches long).
Dressmaker's measure and rule.
Measure book.
Tracing wheel.
Scissors.
Pins.
Adjustable Dress Form (desirable, but not absolutely necessary).

Any of these supplies may be procured from the Academy at reasonable prices.

TAKING MEASUREMENTS

The first and most important requisite for cutting and designing correctly fitted garments is the taking of correct measurements of the figure to be fitted. Therefore, we will assume a set of measurements to be used in our first few lessons, and we would caution you, right here, not to try to make a draft from any other measurements until you thoroughly understand the use of the machine. . For so doing will cause yourself unnecessary work and worry; on the other hand, if you follow the text and illustrations closely you will master the problems very easily. See Plate 2.

MEASUREMENTS IN SAME SEQUENCE

The student should acquire the habit of taking the measurements in the same sequence for each garment, thereby eliminating the necessity for writing the name of the measurement each time they are taken.

Study the illustrations on Plate 2 very carefully and use them continually.

WAIST OR BLOUSE

FRONT measure is taken from just where the collar would go around the neck to the normal waist line. The waist line may always be determined by locating the top of the hip bone and tracing a line on the figure around to the front. Do not be misguided when taking measurements by the particular design worn by the figure being measured.

UNDER=ARM is measured from close under the arm to the waist line or top of hip bone. .

BUST measure. Take the tape in right hand and place around the figure, holding it as high over the shoulder blades as possible, draw it around close up under the arms and across the fullest part of the bust, being careful not to slide the tape on the figure.

CHEST measure is taken as shown on Plate 2, Figure 1, across the chest where the normal armhole seam should appear.

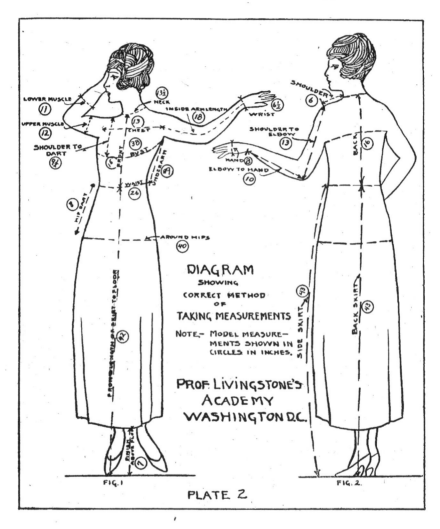

DIAGRAM
SHOWING
CORRECT METHOD
OF
TAKING MEASUREMENTS

NOTE.— MODEL MEASURE-
MENTS SHOWN IN
CIRCLES IN INCHES.

PROF. LIVINGSTONE'S
ACADEMY
WASHINGTON D.C.

FIG. 1   FIG. 2.

PLATE 2

WAIST is measured tight, just above the hip bone or the exact normal waist of the figure.

SHOULDER TO DART. This measurement is taken as shown from the center of the shoulder down to the point of the bust.

SHOULDER is measured from where the collar goes around the neck out to the point of the shoulder.

4

NECK. This measurement is taken just around the neck where a tight collar would fit.

BACK is measured from where the collar goes around the neck down to the small of the back or just where the figure bends.

TWO-SEAM SLEEVE

UPPER MUSCLE. Always measure the right arm and fold the arm back so as to get muscle at full size.

Note.—On Plate 2 the model measurements for you to use are in the circles in inches. The student should practice taking measurements of different size figures, any ladies that may be available, but do not use the measurements for your drawings.

LOWER MUSCLE. This is the largest part of the arm between the elbow and hand.

SHOULDER TO ELBOW. This measurement is taken from the point of the shoulder to the elbow.

ELBOW TO HAND is measured from the point of the elbow to the joint at the wrist.

HAND. Place the tape around the right hand so as it passes over the thumb and largest part of hand.

INSIDE LENGTH. This measurement is taken from the normal armhole seam down the inside of the arm to the wrist, as shown on Plate 2, Figure 1.

SKIRT

HIP. For the average figure about eight inches down from the waist gives the largest part of the hip. You should, however, measure the hip around the figure at the largest point, always noting the distance below the waist line. On stout figures sometimes it is necessary to take the measurement of the hip at two points below the waist, usually eight and twelve inches below.

FRONT LENGTH OF SKIRT. Always measure the length of the skirt from the waist line to the floor front, back and two sides, then deduct from these measurements the distance you desire the skirt finished above the floor. See Plate 2, Figure 1.

MEASURE BOOK

The student should supply herself with a small book for taking and keeping all measurements used. Write the name of the person with the date taken and description of the design to be made. These books may be had from the Academy.

Following is the proper sequence in which the measurements should be taken. The first line is used for the waist proper, the second line is for the sleeve, and the third line is for the skirt measures, hence—

Front,	Under-Arm,	Bust,	Chest,	Waist,	Shoulder to Dart,	Shoulder,	Neck,	Back,
15	9	38	13	26	9½	6	13½	16

Upper muscle,	Shoulder to elbow,	Elbow to hand,	Hand.
12	13	10	8

Waist,	Hip,	Front length,	Sides (R-L),	Back,
26	40	42 minus 7	43	43

LESSON I

ENGLISH BASQUE OR TIGHT FIT DART LINING

Center Front—Sections A-C, Figure 1

Study Plate No. 3 carefully.

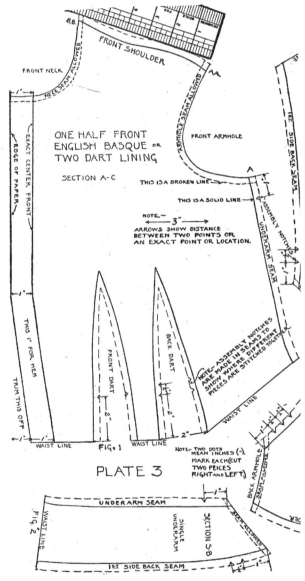

FRONT SHOULDER
FRONT NECK
NECK SEAM ALLOWED
ARMHOLE SEAM ALLOWED
FRONT ARMHOLE
ONE HALF FRONT ENGLISH BASQUE OR TWO DART LINING
SECTION A-C
EXACT CENTER FRONT
EDGE OF PAPER
THIS IS A BROKEN LINE
THIS IS A SOLID LINE
NOTE.— 3" ARROWS SHOW DISTANCE BETWEEN TWO POINTS OR AN EXACT POINT OR LOCATION.
ASSEMBLY NOTCHES
UNDERARM SEAM
1ST SIDE BACK SEAM
THIS 1" FOR HEM
TRIM THIS OFF
FRONT DART
BACK DART
NOTE— ASSEMBLY NOTCHES ARE MADE IN SEAMS TO SHOW WHERE DIFFERENT PIECES ARE STITCHED TOGETHER.
WAIST LINE
FIG. 1
NOTE— TWO DOTS MEAN INCHES (..). MARK EACH (CUT TWO PEICES RIGHT AND LEFT.)
PLATE 3
BACK ARMHOLE SEAM ALLOWED
UNDERARM SEAM
FIG. 2
SINGLE UNDERARM
SECTION S-B
SEAM ALLOWED
1ST SIDE BACK SEAM

Spread your drafting paper (size about 20x30
you on a smooth table or board and place the
A-C of the machine on the paper even with the l

Plate No. 1, Figure 1.)

Set A–C 2, 3 and 4 to length of front 15.

Measure two inches between 3 and 4 at waist line arrow in back dart.

Set A-C 6 to size of bust 38.

Set A-C 5 to length of under-arm nine inches on A-C 6. Then set A-C 5 to 26 waist on A-C 4. It may be necessary to lift A-C 5 slightly to keep fasteners from hanging on the under side.

See that A–C 8, 9 and 11 are pushed down as far as possible so that the 9½ is covered.

Take your scale, place it across the shoulder, slide A–C 9 out to the length of the shoulder 6 inches as shown at AA and BB, Plate No. 3, Figure 1.

Place A–C 10 even with the top of A–C 6. See Plates Nos. 1 and 3, Figure 1A.

Now check over each adjustment you have just made. See that your machine does not move and draw the outline of your front section as shown by heavy lines on Plate 3, Figure 1, down to the waist line and make a dash at each arrow point shown. Remember that the heavy lines indicate the garment and the broken lines show where the seams go.

The student will with a little practice soon become accustomed to using the machine, thereby overcoming the awkwardness at first experienced. You should hold your pencil as nearly straight up or vertical as possible, and place your left hand on each section to hold it steady as you draft the line.

The machine must now be removed from the paper. You will note that the French bust line or true center front has not been drafted, so we will proceed to draft same.. Take the scale in your left hand and, with the square end at the neck curve, measure in from the edge of the paper one inch. Now at the top of the darts, measure in one inch. At the waist line measure in two inches. Now draft a straight line from the first mark you made at the neck to the one at the top of the darts, then draw a slightly curved line from this point to the mark at the waist line. See Plate No. 3, Figure 1. Now at the waist line measure in one inch from the edge of the paper and make a dash, and on the extreme edge of the paper even with the top of the darts make another point; then draw a straight line between these two points. This will give you a triangular piece to be trimmed off.

Seams are allowed at the neck and in the armhole, so draft a broken line to show them. See Plate No. 3, Figure 1. Now draw the seams in the darts, on the shoulder and under-arm and show the assembly notch one inch from the armhole down on the under-arm seam, also in the darts as shown on Figure 1. Then draw waist line as shown in Figure 1. Allowance for seam or hem at waist line is not made in this lesson.

Note.—By "assembly notch" is meant one or more notches cut in the edges of the pieces to show how they are assembled or put together.

This completes the draft for the front section. Now it should have the exact appearance as your Plate No. 3, Figure 1, and if it does not, something is wrong and you should check it over.

Single Under-Arm Section S. B., Figure 2.

The symbol for this section is S–B, and it is made in four parts. Just above the symbol S-B 2 you will see the name printed and above

S-B 1 you will notice two groups of numerals or scales, as they will be called. The upper scale is to be used now at 38. The lower scale is to be used when the double under-arm section is used, as will be explained in detail later on.

For the garment that we are drafting this section is cut separately and stitched to A–C 5 and 6, at the under-arm seam, so we will set it up to the required sizes as follows: Slide S–B 3 to the length of the under-arm, viz., 9. Then slide S–B 4 to the length of the back, viz., 16. Now on the upper or single under-arm scale set S–B 2 to the size of the bust, viz., 38 Now set S–B 4 to the size of the waist, viz., 26. You will note here that 26 is the last numeral on this scale. The lower scale is to be used when you use the double under-arm section D–D.

Now see that the section is set correctly at all four points, bust, waist, under-arm and back. Then draft the outline as given by the section down to the waist line and make a dash at the waist line arrow points. Now show the seam with a broken line on the top end as this is a part of the armhole and the seam is included on the machine. Draw side seams and draw the waist line, which completes this section. Make assembly notches as shown.. See Plate No. 3, Figure 2.

Center Back Section L-L, Figure 3

Place the center back section L–L one-half inch from the left edge of the paper and draft a line, using section L–L 1 as a guide for your pencil. This leaves a seam on the center back. See Plate 3, Figure 3. If we desired the back all in one piece, then we would place the machine on the extreme edge of the paper and draft the pattern, and cut the material on the fold, but for this lesson we will allow a half-inch seam on the center back Set L–L 2 to length of back 16. Set L–L 4 to size of bust 38. You will note that this makes the shoulder the correct 6 inches. Different size shoulders will be treated in the next lesson.

This section is now ready to draft, so draw the outline as given by the machine down to the waist line and make a dash at the arrow-point on both sides. Remove the machine and draw the waist line. Seams are allowed at neck and armhole. Draft them as shown. Also draft shoulder seam and assembly notches as shown on Plate No. 3, Figure 3.

You will notice on Plate No. 1 that the three front sections (Figures 1, 2 and 3) are made for the left side, and the two back sections (Figures 4 and 5) are made for the right side. This is done in order to make them easier to cut. If the back and side back sections L–L and A–D were made the same as the front sections, then we would have to cut lefthanded, which would be very awkward for most persons.

Side Back, Section A-D, Figure 4

Set A–D2 to size of bust 38.

Set A–D 4 to length of back 16 and to size of waist 26. Now draw outline as shown on Plate 3, Figure 4, down to waist line and make dashes. Remove section and draft waist line (always use points of the arrows, never use the feather end). Now draw seams with broken lines and show your assembly notches just as they are on Figure 4.

Double Underarm Section D-D

This section is used for sizes from forty bust and larger, so we will not study its use here. But we will take it up later when we study designs for stout figures.

This completes the first draft for an English Basque or two-dart fitted lining. The student should go over every detail very carefully and be positive that she understands the subject thoroughly. Also place each section of the machine on the draft and see that it is made to the correct measurements, for accuracy is one of the most important requisites in the designing of women's garments, and as the principle of garment making is to fit the figure, we must learn to do this first, then we can make any changes we wish to comply with the styles of the day.

As we have said in a preceding paragraph, we cut only one-half of the design; therefore we must either cut two pieces by each pattern or fold the material and cut it double in order to get the whole garment. It is very important to fold the material either face to face or back to back to be sure that you cut one piece for the right side and one piece for the left side instead of, say, two fronts for the left side when of course one piece would be ruined. See note on Plate 3, Figure 1.

Plain Two-Seam Sleeve, Plates 1 and 4; study them both very carefully.

Measurements required:
Upper Muscle, Shoulder to Elbow, Elbow to Hand, Hand
    12   13   10   8

Place large section T-S of the sleeve close to the lefthand edge of another sheet of paper. Study Plate 1, Figures 6 and 7, and Plate 4. The reference letters apply to both plates.

Set T-S 1 to size of muscle 12. Set lower end to size of hand 8. Now make a dash on the paper opposite the elbow arrow. Plate 1, Figure 6.

Now start to draft from the arrow at elbow to the shoulder up to the 13-inch graduation, and make a dash as shown on Plate No. 1, Figure 6 B3. Then start at the elbow and draft down to the "elbow to hand" measure, viz., 10 B4, and make a dash. Repeat the same operation on the inside from the 13-inch mark B2, at the top, to the 10-inch point B1, near the hand end. Make a dash at both ends of this line as shown on Plate 1, Figure 6.

This leaves both ends open or unfinished. Now slide the sleeve down and connect the two side lines with curved top, keeping sleeve even at point marked B2.. Then connect the bottom or hand end lines with a straight line, B1 and B4. Next draft the seam at the top of the sleeve on the inside and side seams on the outside. Then make assembly notches as shown on Plate 4, Figure 1, and allow one inch hem at hand end.

The small or under side of the sleeve U-S is drafted in the same manner as the top side, but be careful to make section U-S 2 even on the left edge with U-S 3. See Plate No. 1, Figure 7 C2.

Draft the sides and make the dashes at 13 on both sides at the top. C2 and C3, Plate 1, and the same at 10 near the hand C1 and C4. Then make a dash at the elbow arrow. Now draw the machine down and draft the curve for the armhole end. Refer to Plate No. 1, Figure 7. Place the corner CX just so it comes to the end of the line and forms a point at C3 on Plate 4, Figure 2. Then swing the sleeve around until it comes to the end of the line C2 and forms the end of the sleeve. Plate No. 4, Figure 2 C2 and C3. Connect the two lines at the hand end by straight lines C1 and C4. Now draw the one-inch hem at the hand and make assembly notches as shown, also show the seam at the top end and sides. This completes a plain two-seam sleeve. One seam and fancy sleeves will be taken up later on.

The student should now practice over the entire lesson in order to thoroughly understand adjustments. Then draft an entirely new pattern accurately to the same measurements, to be sent in to the Academy for correction and comment.

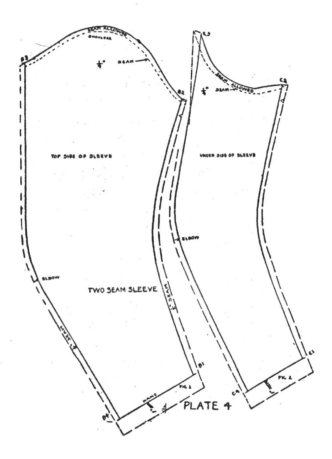

If there is a word, sentence or phrase that you do not fully understand, look it up at once; do not pass it over, as it may be the cause of a great amount of trouble. If you cannot find the exact meaning from the authorities at your command, write in to us immediately stating the location of such words, sentences or phrases, and we will at once define it clearly for you.

Be sure to enclose sufficient postage for return of your lesson, as we cannot keep separate postage accounts for each student.

LESSON II
French Bodice or One-Dart Foundation.
(French Lining)

This design is the foundation for the majority of fitted garments in both dresses and coats and is the most popular and easily fitted design for inner linings.

See Plate No. 5 for illustration and developments.

Place a sheet of paper before you and adjust the front Section A-C of the machine to the measurements just as you did for the English lining in the preceding lesson. Draft the under-arm line as you did in the English lining from armhole to waist line and outline the two darts with a dot and dash line as shown on Plate No. 5, Figure 1.

Now refer to Plates Nos. 1 and 5, Figure 1. You will notice the letter X set in the center of the front dart opposite the waist line arrows. You will indicate the same X on your drawing. Now insert your pencil in the slot marked "top of one dart" and mark full length of slot. See Plate 1, Figure 1 X X.

Do not let the machine move out of position.

At this point we will discuss the proper method for measuring and fitting the neck. To have the shoulder seams to come in the proper place, we shall divide the neck size, 13½ inches, into three equal parts, one third for the back and the other two thirds for the fronts. See Plate No. 5, Figure 2. So we will have one-third of the neck size, or 4½ inches, to measure on the drawing at BB.

Now take the tape measure in your left hand and place the 4½-inch graduation on the true center front line and measure around the neck curve 4½ inches by holding the tape against the curve of the machine, and make a dash. See Plate No. 5, Figure 1 BB.

Set the shoulder sections A-C 8 and 9 to the correct 6 inches and make a dash at top of armhole as shown at AA, Plate 5, Figure 1. Now place A-C 10 in correct position even with the top and edge of A-C 6. See A, Plate 5, Figure 1, and draft the front armhole curve.

You will notice that the 4½-inch marks that you made do not come up to the top of Sections 8 and 9, so we will drop the shoulder Sections A-C 8 and 9 down until they come even with the dashes that you made at the neck BB and Armhole AA. See Plate 5, Figure 1. Now draft the front shoulder line over A C 8 and 9, being sure that the shoulder is set to the proper 6 inches.

Now move the machine to the left so that the arrow on the right side of Section A-C3 comes just to the X you made in the front dart. See Plate No. 1, Figure 1. Now open Section A-C4 as far as it will go and move this dart over on the top until it intersects with the mark you made in the slot "top of one dart." See Plate 1, Figure 1XX. Be sure that Sections A-C 3 and 4 are set to the right front measures, viz., 15 inches. Now draft the one dart as shown by solid line on Plate No. 5, Figure 1.

Remove the machine and transfer the exact front center line just as you did in the preceding lesson. See Plate No. 5, Figure 1.

Now take your scale and measure across the shoulder and locate the center, three inches, and draw a straight line from this point to the top of the dart. See Plate No. 5, Figure 1. Draft the waist line and also the seams as shown on Plate 5, Figure 1. When the two pieces are cut apart on the shoulder to dart line, seams must be allowed also. This completes the draft for the two front sections of a French Lining or Princess Top.

11

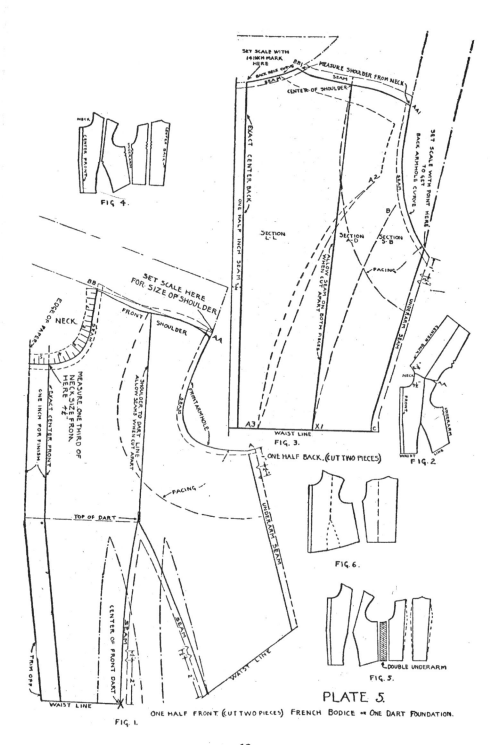

FIG 4.

FIG. 3.

FIG. 2.

ONE HALF BACK. (CUT TWO PIECES)

FIG. 6.

FIG. 5.

DOUBLE UNDERARM

PLATE 5.

ONE HALF FRONT (CUT TWO PIECES) FRENCH BODICE ∞ ONE DART FOUNDATION.

FIG. I.

12

This design may be used with the dart all in one piece if desired, but then it is not a French lining, because the seam must run to the shoulder in a French lining.

Center Back Section

The center back sections L–L should now be set up the same as in the English Lining of the preceding lesson. Draft a broken line all around it from the waist line up on both sides and across shoulder. See Plate No. 5, Figure 3. Be sure to make the dashes at the waist line. Now take the scale and place the 14-inch graduation even with the left edge of the machine at the neck. Be very careful to keep the scale square with the edge of the paper. Now draw around the curve to the 16¼-inch graduation. This is two and a quarter inches, which is one-half of the one-third of the preceding neck size, for we are only making one-half of the back. See Plate 5, Figure 2. Now from the 16¼-inch mark or the end of the curve you just made measure with the scale across the 6 inches for the length of the shoulder, being careful to keep the scale parallel with the broken shoulder line. Now draft heavy shoulder line with Section LL3. See Plate No. 5, Figure 3.

Now remove Section LL of the machine and set up the side back Section A–D to the required measurement just as you did in the English Lining, and place to the right of the center back. Allow the A–D section to come exactly in contact with the draft at the waist line arrows and just touch the curve with the broken line curve at the top. See Plate 1, Figures 4 and 5, and Plate 5, Figure 3, A2 and A3. Now draft the right side of this section with a broken line. See Plate No. 5, Figure 3 BX.

Next set the single under-arm or S–B Section up to the required four sizes, viz., bust, waist, under-arm and back; then reverse it or turn face down and place the waist line arrow in contact with the dash you made at X with the A–D Section and intersect the top with the curve line at the armhole at B. Now draft a solid line for the under-arm to the right of this section down to the waist line and make a dash at C. You will notice that this leaves the back armhole open. Now place your scale with the curved end down and form the back armhole curve as shown by Plate No. 5, Figure 3.. Next measure and locate the center of the shoulder, viz., 3 inches. You will notice that you have three points or lines at the waist line. Now draft a straight line from the point you located on the center of the shoulder down to the center line at the waist, marked X at bottom of Figure 3, Plate 5. Now connect your waist line points and draft seams as shown on Plate No. 5, Figure 3. Draw seams as shown on Figure 3.

Facings

Very often it is required that the sleeves of a dress be stitched to the lining and the armholes of the outer dress are bound or otherwise finished. Whenever this is required it is necessary to put on a facing to prevent the lining from showing around the sleeve, so if you will study Plate 5, Figures 1 and 3, you will see the curved lines around the armhole both front and back. The pattern for this facing which is three inches wide is made by placing a piece of paper under it and tracing the lines through with your tracing wheel. Then the facing pattern will be identical to the lining and will fit perfectly and will not roll up or twist up as you have very likely seen in some dresses.

This completes your draft for the back of a French Lining or Princess Top. Now take your scissors and cut it out and cut the two sections apart. Then place all four sections together and allow all seams, make assembly notches and write the words "center back and center front" along the edges in the proper places as shown on Plate No. 5, Figure 4.

The student should practice over the lesson at least three times and be sure to understand it thoroughly, as this French Lining or Princess Top is really the hardest point to master, and when once understood thoroughly furnishes the foundation for the majority of fitted garments.

After you understand it thoroughly draft another pattern to the same measurements, cut it out and send in to the Academy for correction and comment.

When finished, you drawing should have the exact appearance of Plate No. 5, Figure 4.

Bear in mind that on the pattern the front is made on the left side and the back is made on the right side. Therefore, when placed together as in Figure 4, the back pieces must be turned opposite to the way they were drafted.

French Lining or Princess Top for Stout Figures.

This design is for figures where the bust size is 41 and over and the waist size is 26 and over. You will note on Section A–C 4, that the waist measure scale is only numbered to 26, but by counting to the edge of the section you see that it can be used up to a 30 waist without the double under-arm Section D–D. So you do not use the double under-arm D–D for sizes smaller than a forty bust and thirty waist.

We will assume the following measurements for a stout figure and make a French Lining or Princess Top to fit:

Front	Underarm	Bust	Chest	Waist	Shoulder to Dart	Shoulder	Neck	Back
16	9	42	15	30	10½	6½	14	16

You should transfer these measurements to your measure book for later reference.

Set up the Front Section A–C the same as you did in the preceeding lesson except you set the bust size out as far as it will go and set the waist size to the last measurement which is 26.

Note carefully the change in all measurements and set the machine section A–C just as you have learned in the preceeding lessons and draft the front sections of the pattern as shown on Plate 5, Figure 1. being carful as to accuracy.

It is very necessary to have the chest measure the right size especially for stouts, so be careful to set A–C 10 so that you get the required 7½ inches from the center front to the armhole.

Double Under-arm Section D-D

This Section D–D is used for designs of 41 bust size or larger. And the better practice is to set it up to the required sizes just as you have learned to set the single under-arm and side-back sections, then make a separate piece and set it in with seams between the front (Figure 1) and the back Figure 3 (See Figure 5).

If it is desirable this section can be added half to the front and half to the back. See the dotted line in center of Double Under-Arm piece, Plate No. 5, Figure 5, thereby having only one seam under the arm instead of two. This necessitates making both the back and front pieces just the width of half of this piece wider.

In this stout model that you are making, the single under-arm S–B and the side back A–D Sections are set to the required sizes on the lower or double under-arm scale for the bust and waist measurements, and they are used exactly the same as in the preceeding lessons.

The center back section is used identically the same in this lesson as in the preceeding one except that the measurements are for a different size.

When making a pattren for extra stout figures it is usually necessary to spring out a little over the shoulder as shown by the dotted lines on Figure 5.

Plain Lining

This lining is made in just three pieces by not cutting the princess lines in it and by leaving in the dart. The under-arm seams on the front and back are just as in the Princess Top. Refer to Plate 5, Figure 6 and you will readily see the development.

LESSON III

Plain Waist or Blouse

In this lesson we will take up and develop a plain waist or blouse. We will use the measurements that we used in the first lesson.

A plain waist may be open at any desired location. The center back. center front and under the left arm being the three most popular places. They may be either buttoned, hooked or snapped.

To make a pattern for a plain waist to open down the center front.

Place a sheet of paper in front of you and set up the Front Section A-C of the machine just as you did for the French Lining or Princess Top, in Lesson No. 2.

This design will be made without darts and the back will be cut on the fold. See Plate No. 6, Figures 1 and 2.

The bust and waist will be set two sizes larger on all sections. That is, Bust 38 plus 2 equals 40 and the waist 26 plus 2 equals 28. This is for looseness and must be increased or decreased according to the style of garment and the taste of the wearer. Move Section A-C 6 out as far as it will go at the bust and set the waist A-C 5 to the second graduation on the waist scale that is not numbered. This is 28. The back dart is set with the same two inches, and this extra material caused by the darts is left in to cause the waist to blouse, and if so much blouse is not desired you may redraft the underarm line made by A-C 5 and 6 a little straighter down, that is, draw it in at the waist until you get the desired fullness. See Plate No. 6, Figure 1 A-AB.

The center front line is drafted straight down to the waist line as shown on Plate No. 6, Figure 1. Be very careful to have your chest measurement correct. This is governed by moving A-C 10 in or out as shown at AA and A on Plate 6, Figure 1.

After you have the Front Section set up, check your neck and shoulder measuresments very carefully then check the other measurements, if correct, draft to your paper down to the waist line only and make the dashes at the waist line arrows as usual.

For the back we will set up the center back Section L-L and the side back Section A-D just as we did for the French Lining except allow two sizes larger than the measurements at the bust and waist, that is a 40 bust and 28 waist on the upper or single under-arm scale. Now draft these sections with a broken line just as you did on the French Lining. See Plate No. 6, Figure 2. Now take your single under-arm Section S-B and set it to the required sizes allowing two sizes larger at the bust and waist on the upper or single under-arm scale then reverse it (turn face down) and add it to the other two sections. keeping the waist points even just as you did in the French Lining. See Plate No. 6, Figure 2. Now check up the measurement on all sections and draft all three sections all in one piece, just as you did for the French Lining. See Plate No. 6, Figure 2.

You will see that this leaves the arm-hole irregular and unfinished, so take your scale and place the 18-inch mark at the bottom of the arm-hole and bring the upper part in contact until it reaches the end of the shoulder then draw the back arm-hole just as you did in a French Lining. See Plate No. 6, Figure 2. Then draw the underarm seam line straight down which gives the looseness for blouse back.

See Plate 6, Figures 1 and 2. Take your scale and extend the underarm, Lines A1 and A2, center front B1 and B2, and center back lines C1 and C2 down three inches below the waist. This is for the finish to be worn either over or under the skirt.

Plain Waist or Blouse for Stout Figures

For a plain waist sizes above 40 bust, set all bust and waist measurements two sizes larger than actual measurements. Use the Double-Under-Arm and develop just as you did the stout French Lining. See Plate 6, Figure 4 A, B, C. Use the same measurements as you did for the Stout French Lining exept allow for looseness at bust and waist. Study Plate No. 6, Figure 4 carefully to get the quickest results.

Figure 3 shows method of changing shoulder seam. This is done by placing the shoulders of the back and front patterns together and drawing another line as far down the front as desired for a yoke or drop shoulder as it is sometimes called. See Figure 3, AA. If a separate yoke is desired, as in a shirt, this may be made by drawing the line shown at BB also. This gives three pieces. After drawing the lines to show the changes place another piece of paper under the pattern and trace all lines through to the underside, them remove and cut apart and allow seams.

When extra fullness for a plait or tucks or gathers is desired. cut the front pattern apart and spread it out until the required fullness is obtained and then cut the material or another pattern with the extra fullness in it as shown at K and K1 on Figure 4.

The difference between a plain waist or blouse and a shirt waist is that the latter has a yoke on the shoulder and should have a one-seam sleeve with a cuff. See Plate No. 7 for illustration and details.

Surplice or Crossover Blouse

Refer to Plate 6, Figure 7A. Fold your paper through the center then use this folded edge for the center front and draw a regular plain waist or blouse as you have learned to do; now transfer the outline through to the under side with your tracing wheel, unfold the paper, you have the entire front before you, Figure 7B. Now measure down the center front from the neck to X, which for this design we make 9 inches. Now start at the end of the right shoulder X1 and draft the curved surplice line over to the waist line on the left side X2, being careful to let the curve pass through the right point X on the center. Refold your paper on the center front and transfer the X and X1 line to the left side. This will give you X and X3. Now unfold and measure out on the right shoulder 3½ inches to X4. This will give the outside of the collar. Now cut the back of a plain waist, place the shoulders together as shown at X1 and X5, then measure down the center back 4 inches and draw the outside line of the collar from X8 through X4 and down to X2; in drawing this free hand curve lay your hand flat on the paper and with a light broken line form the shape until you get it right, then draw the line solid. Now place a separate piece of paper under the drawing and trace the collar through to it and mark center back, cut on fold and allow seams.

Draw the line X7 2 inches below the neck. This gives the top of pattern for the vest.

The whole pattern must now be cut apart on the line X1–X and X2, then the line X3 to X. The line X2, X4 and X8 is not cut as that is made only to get the shape of the collar which will be perfectly flat on the blouse; if you want the collar to roll make the lines from X4 to X8 and X1 to X9 straight instead of curved. Always allow seams when you cut two pieces of a design apart.

If desired the left side may be extended down to full length, then it would appear just as Figure 5.

Fancy Blouse Development

To make any fancy blouse, a plain or master pattern must be made first, then the lines of design drawn in it, which is then cut apart into the separate pieces and seams allowed.

On Plate 6, Figure 6, is shown a plain Peter Pan or flat collar, and

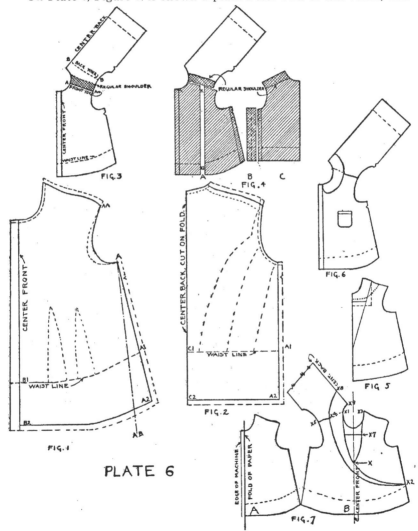

PLATE 6

this is developed just as you did the facings for the sleeves on linings. When a collar, bertha, facing, pocket or any trimming must lie flat on the garment, the pattern must be outlined on the original pattern

17

first and then transferred to another piece of paper and cut out, allowing seams.

Plate 6, Figure 5, shows a plain V-neck blouse that leaves 2½ inches of the shoulder bare and a vest that leaves 2 inches of the front neck bare.

The round, square and other necks are developed in the same manner by locating the point desired on the shoulder and then the distance you wish the neck bare in front, then connect the two points with a line of the desired shape square, round or otherwise, as shown by the broken and dotted lines on Figure 5.

LESSON IV

Plain One-Seam Sleeve

The measurements to be used are as follows: Upper muscle, 12; length of seam, 18; width of cuff, 8. See Plate No. 3 for illustration of terms.

Remember that the measurements that we took are tight. Now we will make allowance for looseness to conform to the style and also to comfort to the wearer.

We will allow two inches for looseness at the upper muscle, a cuff 8 inches long or around the wrist and three inches wide; allow two inches or more on the bottom width of sleeve proper, for gathering into the cuff. See Plate No. 7, Figure 2, and note carefully so that you understand the terms thoroughly.

Now draft a one-seam sleeve with cuff to the measurements assumed above. These measurements should be placed in your measure book under the heading "Measurements for one-seam sleeve."

Take a sheet of paper and fold it through the center the long way. See Plate 7, Figures 1 H and F1. This will give you a double sheet. Now lay the folded sheet in front of you with the folded edge towards you. The folded edge represents the center of the sleeve from a line at the top of the armhole at the shoulder point.

Remember that we lay out and develop one-half of the sleeve first, and then unfold the paper, so all of the measurements around the arm must be divided in half. Note this carefully. Study Plate 7, Figure 1, carefully.

Take your scale and measure from the lefthand end of the paper on the folded edge and make a mark at 8 inches, Figure 1A. This is a construction point only and you will learn later why you made it. Now from this point A turn your scale across the paper at right angle with the folded edge and measure one-half of the muscle, viz., 6 inchess to A1. Then from this point measure one-half of the fullness required B, which is one inch more or 7 inches from the folded edge of the paper to B. This gives the seam edge at the upper muscle.

Now place your scale with the square end to the left and the three-inch graduation on the last point you made at B for the muscle, slant the scale about two inches towards the folded edge of the paper at the bottom of the sleeve; now make a mark at the top or square end of the scale C and at the 18-inch graduation D or the other end of the scale for the full length of the sleeve. Now make a mark at the 15-inch graduation E. This is to deduct the three inches for the cuff, and it gives you the net length of the sleeve without the cuff. Opposite the 15-inch graduation E measure across the sleeve from the folded edge E one-half of the cuff size, viz., 4 inches, and add one-half of the allowance for gathers, viz., one inch, making the sleeve 5 inches in width at the bottom from E to F1. Now draw a

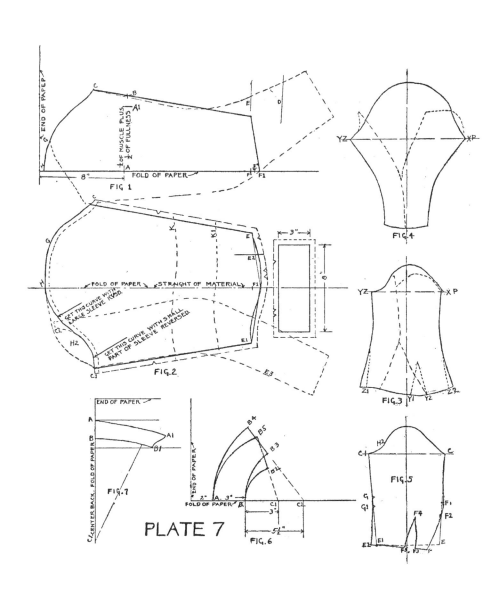

FIG 1
END OF PAPER
C
B
A1
¼ OF MUSCLE PLUS, ½ OF FULLNESS
E
D
A
8"
FOLD OF PAPER
F2 F1

FIG.2
C
G
K
K1
E
E2
FOLD OF PAPER
STRAIGHT OF MATERIAL
F1
3"
8
H
GET THIS CURVE WITH LARGE SLEEVE ROD.
GET THIS CURVE WITH SMALL PART OF SLEEVE REVERSED.
C2
H2
E1
C1
E3

FIG.4
YZ
XP

FIG.3
YZ
XP
Z1
Y1
Y2
Z2

FIG.7
END OF PAPER
A
B
A1
B1
CENTER BACK. FOLD OF PAPER

FIG.6
END OF PAPER
B4
B5
B3
B2
2"
A
3"
FOLD OF PAPER
B
C1
C2
3"
5½"

FIG.5
H2
C1
C
G
G1
F1
F2
F4
E1
E2
F3
E

PLATE 7

straight line from this point E to the point you made at the top of the scale C, being sure to draw through the mark B you made for the the seam less the cuff, which is 15 inches. See Plate No. 7, Figure 1. size of the muscle plus the fullness. This line gives the full length of

To get the right shape at the hand end of the sleeve, take your scale in the right hand and hold it at right angles with the folded edge of the paper F. Now measure down three fourths of an inch to F1, then take your scale and draw the bottom of the sleeve from E to F1 with just a little curve at the folded edge. This completes the back half of the plain sleeve. Now with your tracing wheel trace the lines through to the under side of your paper, being very careful to follow the lines accurately.

After carefully tracing all lines through to the under side unfold the paper and you will have the full sleeve before you, Figure 2, but the top on the front side must be eased out or shaped H2 to throw the sleeve more to the front when it is sewn into the armhole. This is necessitated by the present style and may be changed any season. (In fact, this style is just the opposite of the regular custom. That is, the shaped out part of the sleeve is usually placed under the arm and the seam of sleeve is placed two inches on the front from the under arm seam, but the present style is to shape out the front and let the seam of the sleeve come directly to the under-arm seam of the waist.)

To get the shape to be eased out set up the small Section U-S of the machine to the size of the muscle and reverse it. That is, turn face down and place on or as near parallel as possible with the edge of the sleeve as shown by broken line C1 and E3, then draft the top curve about one-third around C1 to C2. See Plate No. 7, Figure 2.

Then place the large section T-S even with the line on the top at H, move it over to the curve you have just made and complete the reverse curve. See Plate No. 7, Figure 2, H and C1.

Bear in mind that the shaped out part of the sleeve H2 is the front.

Now take your scale and at the bottom of the sleeve on the back at E measure over two inches and make a mark E2, then draft a line two inches long. This is to be slashed and faced for the placket, which is to give plenty of room for the hand to pass through. Now draft seams and assembly notches as shown on Plate No. 7, Figure 2. To shape the bottom end of this modern one-seam sleeve divide the width into four parts and shape the curve as shown at E F1 and E1 by the solid line.

The broken lines K and K1 indicate the length for half or three-fourth length sleeves.

If the instructions are followed closely and accurately there should be no trouble in assembling the sleeve to the armhole, but as a precaution it is well to measure the entire armhole with your tape and then measure the top of the sleeve around the curve; it is customary to ease the sleeve into the armhole a little and it may be from ¾ of an inch to 1½ inches larger than the armhole, and this material may be eased in; but if there is more than this difference, then the armhole must be eased out a little or the sleeve may be trimmed down a little on the muscle lines, starting at nothing at E and E1 and trimming slightly up to C and C1.

This completes the plain one-seam sleeve, from which design the majority of the variations and fancy sleeves are developed.

The cuff is a plain piece cut 3 inches wide and 8 inches long with seams allowed.

Sleeve Variations

The development of sleeves to make the many shapes and designs seems to be a difficult task for most beginners, the reason being simply because they do not realize that the plain foundation must be made first and then the design developed therefrom.

We will take up the development of the important designs to show the simple method of drafting them.

On Plate 7, Figure 3, is shown the Bell Sleeve, which means that it is flared out like a bell at its lower edge. This may be done in a varying degree as style and taste dictate. This design is made by setting the two sections of the sleeve to the desired muscle size and placing them together at the top or armhole end, then overlapping or opening the lower or hand end until the desired bell is obtained. Then measure the inside or seam length as you do on the regular one-seam sleeve and connect the hand ends with a curved line.

The Bishop Sleeve, so called because it was first used on the robe of bishops, is made the same as the bell sleeve, then shirred or gathered into a cuff or band at the wrist. Another style is to shape in at the hand with a dart at Y1 and Y2 and straightening the seam lines as shown by the dotted lines, Figure 3, Z1 and Z2.

The Leg o' Mutton sleeve receives its name because it is in general appearance the shape of a leg of mutton. It is one of the oldest definite sleeve designs that we have and becomes quite popular from time to time. It is made on the same principle as the bell sleeve except that the extra fullness is at the shoulder and is shirred or gathered into the armhole as the bell is at the cuff.

Plate 7, Figure 4, shows the development. Place the two sleeve sections together at the hand end, flare the top out to the desired size, then from the end with an easy curve as shown on Figure 4. This curve may be made high or low as the design requires. It is very important to see that the points XP and YZ are on a straight line across so that in assembling the two sides the seam will come together and the sleeve will not twist on the arm.

One=Seam Fitted Sleeve, shown on Figure 5, becomes very popular from time to time as the styles change.

To develop the sleeve, first cut a plain one-seam sleeve to the measurements required, then pin this pattern to another piece of paper and develop as follows:

Note that C, C1, E and E1 are the corners of the plain one-seam sleeve as shown on Figure 2. The most important change on this sleeve is that the line C–E is curved over to the left, making the distance from E to F 2 inches and the same line, C–E, 2 inches longer to F.

The distance between F1 and F2 is 4 inches and between G and G1 is 2 inches, so we fold a plait in the line C–F at F1 and F2 to make it the same length as the other side, C1 and Ea. The line G1 and E2 is curved out just 1 inch from E1, which gives the sleeve a little twist to keep it from twisting on the arm.

The dart is cut out to make the desired size at the wrist, this is measured from E2 to F5 and from F3 to F cutting out any unnecessary material and shaping with just a little curve up to the largest part of the lower muscle at F4.

It is important to keep the ends of the sides even or straight across C and C1, then fold the long side Cf into a plait at F1 and F2 to make the two sides the same length when stitched and to have plenty of room at the elbow, while also fitting the lower arm.

20

The front side of the top H2, Figure 2 should not be curved out so much in this design as in the plain sleeve.

Circular and Ripple Cuffs

Plate 7, Figure 6, shows the development of two circular cuffs. We will discuss and develop one here.

Fold your paper as you did for the one seam sleeve and measure 2 inches from the end on the folded edge and make a mark at A on Figure 6, from this point A measure 3 inches for the width of the cuff to B, from B measure to C2 5½ inches.

Take a stout pin and stick it into your paper and board at the point C2, tie a loop on a piece of thread and hook the loop over the pin, then hold your pencil on B and wrap the thread around it, then draw the curve B to B3 allowing the thread to guide your pencil. Now draw the outside or A to B4 line in the same manner.

Now measure from B to B3 the length of half of your cuff 5 inches and maek a mark at B3, and draw a line from C2, through B3 to B4.

The other cuff shown on Figure. A, B, B2 and B5, is developed in the same manner as above. To get more circle to the cuff move the C1 closer to B and to make less circle move it farther away, always keeping on the folded edge and always making the distance from B to B2 or B3, equal to half of the sleeve size at lower end.

Roll Collars

The Roll Collar is developed on the same principle as the circular cuff, the main difference being that the distance from the inside of the collar B on Figure 7 to C1 is much greater because the curve must be much straighter.

The end of the collar outside edge A to A1 may be made any desired shape.

Contrary to the principle governing the cuffs, on the collar the straighter the line B—B1 is, the more the collar will roll and the more the B—B1 line curves the flatter the collar will lie.

LESSON V

Kimona Waist or Blouse

The kimona foundation is used for the design of many garments; street, afternoon and evenings gowns as well as negilgees. Every season brings variations of detail that none can forecast.

You will study in this lesson the development of the two most important outlines and some of the fancy details with which you will have a working knowledge so as to advance with the change of style each season brings.

The most generally used design is shown on Plate 8, Figure 3, and another design is shown on Figure 4.

We will develop Figure 4 first , which has a seam on the shoulder from neck to the end of the sleeve, as shown. The plain sleeve development is shown on Figure 3.

We will proceed to develop a plain kimona waist or blouse as shown on Figure 4. Lay out, draft and cut out a pattern for a plain blouse as you have already learned to do and place the back and front with the shoulder points together at the neck as shown on Plate 8, Figure 1, raise the front shoulder E1 up three-fourths of an inch to E2 and place the scale with the 13-inch mark at E2 and allow the curve of scale to fit shoulder curve; then extend top line of the front of the sleeve E2 to F, being careful to keep the line straight when **you** move the scale along to make the full length of the sleeve, which for this lesson is 18 inches from AH to F, so draft the E2 to F

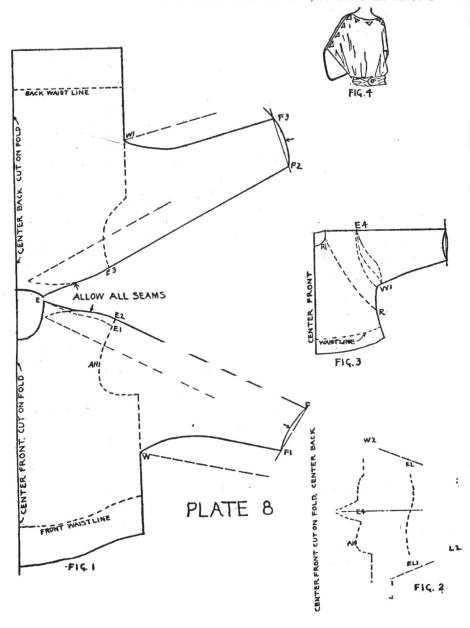

FIG. 4

BACK WAIST LINE

CENTER BACK CUT ON FOLD

F3

W1

F2

E3

E

ALLOW ALL SEAMS

E2

E1

AHI

CENTER FRONT. CUT ON FOLD

FRONT WAISTLINE

FIG. I

PLATE 8

W

FI

F

E4

R1

CENTER FRONT

W1

R

WAISTLINE

FIG. 3

CENTER FRONT CUT ON FOLD, CENTER BACK

W2

EL

E4

AH

ELI

L2

FIG. 2

line long enough to make this; then measure from AH straight over to F, 18 inches.

The under-arm length on the plain waist foundation is 8 inches

22

2

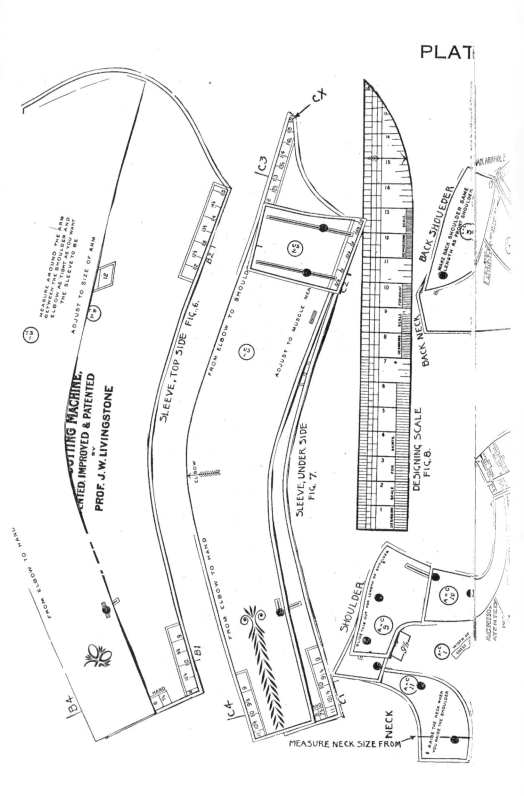

PLAT

cx

C3

SLEEVE, TOP SIDE FIG. 6.

FROM ELBOW TO SHOULDER

SLEEVE, UNDER SIDE FIG. 7.

ADJUST TO MUSCLE MEAS

C2

CUTTING MACHINE, ENTED, IMPROVED & PATENTED

BY

PROF. J. W. LIVINGSTONE

MEASURE AROUND THE ARM BETWEEN THE SHOULDER AND ELBOW AS TIGHT AS YOU WANT THE SLEEVE TO BE

ADJUST TO SIZE OF ARM

T.S.1

B2

ELBOW

FROM ELBOW TO HAND

B1

HAND

B4

FROM ELBOW TO HAND

C4

C1

HAND

MEASURE NECK SIZE FROM

NECK

RAISE THE NECK WHEN YOU RAISE THE SHOULDER

SHOULDER

SLIDE THIS OUT FOR LENGTH OF SHOULDER

A C 9

A C 10

A C 7

A C 8

WIDTH OF CHEST

BACK SHOULDER

MAKE BACK SHOULDER SAME LENGTH AS FRONT SHOULDER

BACK NECK

BACK ARMHOLE

DESIGNING SCALE FIG. 8.

USE FOR 40" BUST AND LAR

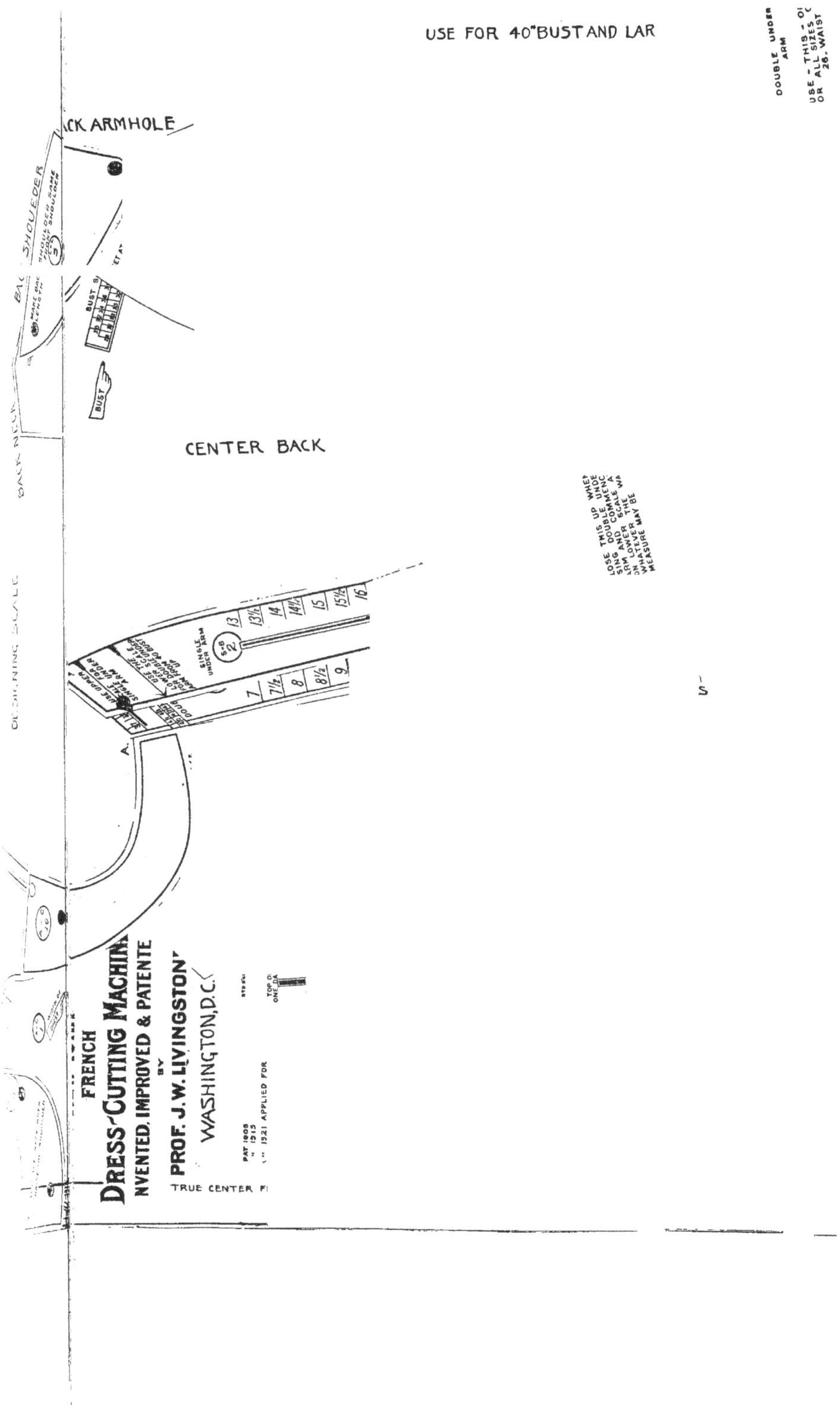

DOUBLE UNDER ARM

USE - THIS - OI OR ALL SIZES C 26. WAIST

CK ARMHOLE

BACK SHOULDER

BUST O

CENTER BACK

SINGLE UNDER ARM

13½
14
14½
15
15½
16

7
7½
8
8½
9

FRENCH
DRESS-CUTTING MACHIN
NVENTED, IMPROVED & PATENTE
BY
PROF. J. W. LIVINGSTON
WASHINGTON, D.C.

PAT 1908
1915
1921 APPLIED FOR

TRUE CENTER F

TOP O
ON

and we start the kimona sleeve 3½ inches above the waist line W. So next measure down from F the size of the sleeve at the wrist (8 inches); one-half is 4 inches, from F to F1. Now place the point of the scale at W and draw the bottom line of the sleeve to F1. To finish the curve at the hand, place the 13-inch mark of the scale at F and the 17-inch mark at F1 and draw the concave curve.

To develop the back of the sleeve, turn the scale face down and place the 12-inch mark at E3; let it fit the curve of the shoulder and draw the line E3 to F2. Be careful to keep the line straight when you move the scale to the full length, which is the same as E2 to F, 17 inches. Now measure from F2 to F3, 4 inches, for the end of the sleeve, and draw the bottom line from W1 to F3 with the point of the scale at W1, as shown. Get the convex curve on the back of the sleeve with the 13-inch mark of the scale at F2 and 17-inch mark at F3. The waist here is shown with a 3-inch over blouse from the waist line. This is a design that is very popular at times, although it is rather close for one having to raise the arms to any extent, as the blouse must slide up from the waist when the arms are raised.

The curve under the arm may be changed to any desired shape to suit the individual, either made from or below the waist line or made to spring from closer under the arm.

Figure 3 shows several designs of kimona. The development is similar to the one you just completed except the pattern is made for half of the design without a seam on the shoulder, and the material is folded through the center front and center back and only the under-arm and sleeves are to be stitched, which is done in one continuous seam. In the foundation the sleeves are not cut separately, but if desired they may be cut apart and seams allowed, then stitched back into the armhole, as shown on Plate 8, Figure 3, E4 and W1.

Proceed to develop the plain kimona with no shoulder seams. First prepare a plain waist pattern to the measurements used on the other kimona. Use the edge of your paper for the center front and center back line. Place the foundation pattern as shown on Figure 2 and develop as follows: Be careful to keep the shoulder points together at E. Now draw the straight line for the shoulder and top of the sleeve, E to E1. Measure from W to W1 on the under-arm line, 3 inches, and make a mark as shown; measure from AH to E1, the length of the seam, 18 inches, and draw a straight line, LI and L2; then measure from E1 to L1, 5 inches, and from E1 to L2, 6 inches, and draw both curves with the point of the scale at E1; this is to give the proper shape at the wrist.

Now draw seam of sleeve, W1 to L2 and from W2 to LI, using the scale with the point at W1 and W2 as shown. The line EL and EL1 shows a shorter length sleeve, and this can be made any length desired, with the curve shaped as at L1, E1 and L2.

Figure 3 shows a front view of this waist, the line W1 to E4 showing the method for cutting out the sleeve in order to set it back with a seam or to use a different material. Place the point of the scale at W1 and draw the line up to E4, then trace the line through to the underside or back, cut out and shape as shown by the dotted line W1 to E4. Then allow seams on both the sleeve and waist.

The same principle applies to the raglan sleeve as to the one on the end of the shoulder.

The raglan sleeve is shaped from any desired point on the underarm line to the desired point on the shoulder or neck, as shown by the line R and R1.

Plain Coat, Double Breasted

This design is made on the same lines as the French Lining or Princess Top and the development is very nearly the same, as you see on Plate 9, Figure 5.

Paste two sheets of paper together and place the machine at the left hand end but place it just two inches over from the edge, as shown on Plate No. 9, Figure 1, A–A.

For the top part, above the waist line set the machine up exactly as you do for the French Lining or Princess Top, except that you set the bust and waist measurements two (2) sizes larger than the actual measurement. This is for the necessary fullness for a coat and is increased or decreased according to the looseness desired. The lines are developed the same as the French Lining or Princess Top down to the waist line and for the skirt portion we develop as follows: The exact center front line is extended straight down to the required length, in this case 8 inches below the waist to H, then all of the other lines H1 to H7 are continued down on the same curve, or are moved in or out as desired to give the required size at the hip.

It is very important to check the hip size on the lines H, H1, H2, H3, H4, H5, H6 and H7. This should be just half of the coat size at the hip and should be three or more inches larger than the hip measurement. Note dot and dash lines B1, B2, B3 and B4 on Plate No. 9, Figure 1, and on Figure 3, C1, C2, C3 and C4. These show how to get the desired hip size.

Now we will develop the rever or lapel. the neck line C is continued straight over to the edge of the paper CC as shown on Plate No. 9, Figure 1. The point A3 is raised one-half inch from CC, this may be more or less according to the design. Now, the rever is folded back to the desired distance down the front or three inches above the waistline, D, and the upper end is folded so it comes directly into neck curve E and a straight line drawn from E to C. See Plate No. 9, Figure 1.

The first button is always placed even with the end of the rever or just where it begins to roll at D and the balance are placed as desired below this point. The facing line and where canvass goes is shown on Figure 5.

For a design that required a dart from the bust to the shoulder without full length seam use the foundation in Figure 5. Place the front of pattern together at the bust and close it together at the bottom H1 and H2. This gives the dart above the bust.

The back may be cut all in one piece by placing the two back pieces in Figure 5 together and cutting the material on the fold at the center back.

For a plain or fancy box coat place the foundation as in Figure 5 and draw the under-arm lines straight down to desired size at the hip, disregarding the dart entirely.

It is plain to be seen that a figure with a prominent bust cannot wear a box coat without a dart as it would stand out in the front instead of hanging straight down.

To draft the collar we place the back and front sections together at the shoulder seam as shown on Plate 9, Figure 5 and measure around from the center back F through the point F1 to the point FF; this gives 7½ inches. Now we lay off the collar from the center back as shown on Plate No. 9, Figure 6.

Let the edge of your paper be the center back, draw a straight line F and FF, measure from F to F1 5 inches and to FF, 2½ inches more, draw the end of the collar 2 inches from FF to F2; now on the center back line

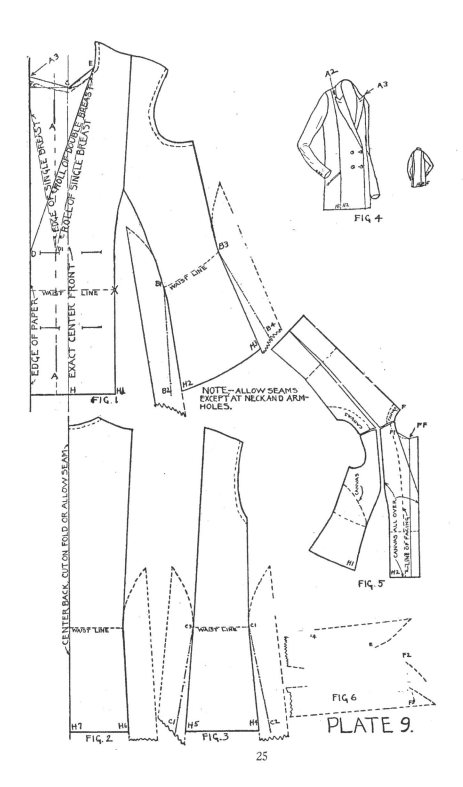

A3

E

EDGE OF SINGLE BREAST

EDGE OF DOUBLE BREAST

EDGE OF SINGLE BREAST

A

D

EXACT CENTER FRONT

WAIST LINE

EDGE OF PAPER

A

H   H1

FIG. 1

B1   WAIST LINE   B3

B2   H2

B4

H3

NOTE — ALLOW SEAMS
EXCEPT AT NECK AND ARM-
HOLES.

A2   A3

FIG 4

CENTER BACK, CUT ON FOLD OR ALLOW SEAM

WAIST LINE

H7   H6

FIG. 2

C1   WAIST LINE   C1

C3   WAIST LINE   C1

C1   H5   H4   C2

FIG. 3

CANVAS

CANVAS

F

F1

PF

CANVAS ALL OVER

LINE OF FACING

H1

H2

FIG. 5

E4

E

F2

FIG 6

F3

PLATE 9.

25

measure from F to F3 the outside stand of the collar 2 inches, and from F3 to F4 measure 1½ inches for the inside stand, next draw the curved line from F2 to F4 with the 16-inch mark on your scale at F2. Now transfer the point at F1 up to E and draw the curved line with the 15-inch mark on your scale at E, from E to F3. This gives the line where the collar turns over. Now shape the outside of the collar with the 16-inch mark of your scale on FF over to F. The line F2 to F5 should be made closer or further from FF according to the space desired between the end of the collar and the end of the rever. See A2 on Figure 4.

Coat, Single Breasted

To change this design to a single breasted coat extend the line AA on Figure 1 all the way down which gives the edge of your coat. move the line D in until it comes on the line AA and draw this roll line to E as in the Double Breasted design. Then shape off the outside of the rever with a line slightly curved at the top from CC to D1 on the line AA.

You have already learned to make the plain two seam sleeve in Lesson 1.

LESSON VII

Plain Two-Piece Skirt

A plain two-piece skirt is cut with the seams on the sides of the figure or the continuation of the under-arm seam of the waist, therefore, we cut the pattern one-half of the front and one-half of the back so the material is cut on the fold, center front and center back making two pieces.

The measurements required for the skirt are the waist, hip, front length, two side lengths and back length; all measurements for the length of the skirt are taken from the waist line to the floor and then deduct from this the distance the skirt is finished above the floor, plus the allowance for the hem.

If your paper is too small paste two sheets together on the long way This will give you a sheet 36 by 48 inches or larger. Now place the skirt machine on the edge of the paper as shown on Plate No. 10, Figure 1.

The measurements for this skirt we will assume to be, waist 26, hip 40, front length 42, sides 43 and back 43. These measurements are to the floor and we wish the skirt finished 7 inches from the floor so they would appear in your measure book as follows:
26   40   42 — 7   43   43   (Note the minus 7 after the front length)

We draft the pattern for one-half of the skirt and that half will be in two pieces. The first thing we must do is to determine the size of each piece at the different points so we will divide the waist 26 into four parts which is 6½ inches on the front at the waist, we move the seam points one into toward the back so we add one inch to this which makes the waist of our skirt pattern 7½ inches for the front quarter from C to C2. This one inch is added to make the seam come in the right place on the side.

The hip measure is 40 inches and we divide this into four parts which makes it 10 inches and we add one-half inch at the hip for comfort and ease over the front of the thigh. This makes the hip measure in the front 10½ inches. Now at the hem we must determine the amount of material required in the bottom of the skirt this depends to a great extent upon the style in vogue and the hip size. So for this lesson we will use 2 yards for the whole skirt at the hem line. This being reduced gives us 72 inches and divide this by four we get 18 inches for the width of the pattern at the hem both back and front. Now see that your machine is placed correctly according to Plate No. 10, Figure 1, C and C1. and draw around the waist curve to the 6½ inch mark C to C1 and make a dash, then 1 inch more or

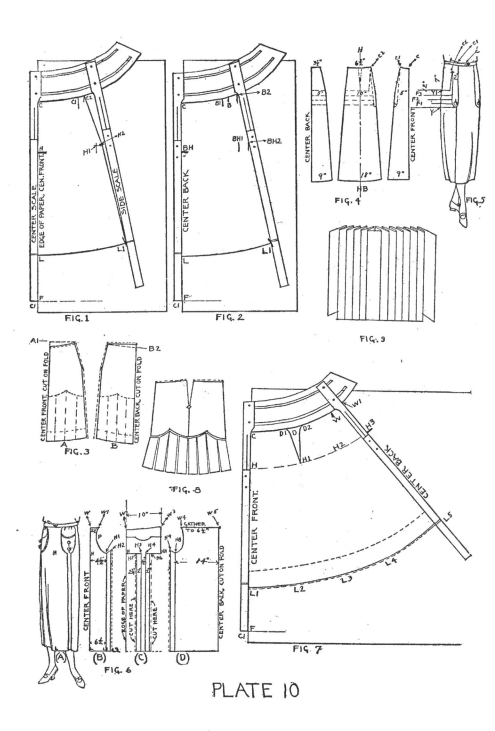

FIG.1

FIG.2

FIG.4

FIG.5

FIG.9

FIG.3

FIG.8

FIG.6

FIG.7

PLATE 10

27

7½ inches to C2 as shown. Now for the hip, measure down on the edge of the paper 8 inches C to H and also measure down 8 inches from C2 to H2. This is to give the length of the dart for the hip. Now from this 8 inch mark on the edge of the paper H measure over the one-fourth of the hip size 10 inches to H1, plus the one-half inch, viz., 10½ inches from H to H2; next set the center front scale to the length of the front of the skirt, viz., 42 inches at F and measure up 7 inches to L. Now measure over the one-fourth of the size of the skirt at the hem, viz., 18 inches to LI and make a long dash, now set the side scale which is the side seam, to the length of the side, which is 43 inches. Now place the side scale on the 18 inch dash at L1 and draft a line up to the hip point H2 and from this point draft the side of the dart to C2 at the waist curve. This gives you the front half of the skirt. The back is drafted in the same manner except we deduct the 1 inch, that we add on the front at the waist line, then we add three inches for gathers at the waist line and add one and half inches at the hip for fullness and develop as follows. Refer to Figure 2, Plate 10—place the machine on the edge of the paper C and C1 as you did to draft the front, draw around on the curve to 6½ inches and then take off the one inch that you added to the front which gives you 5½ inches at B1. Now from B1 5½ inches add 3 inches for gathers which gives you 8½ inches from C to B2.

Now measure from C to BH 8 inches, and from B2 to BH2, 8 inches, then measure from BH to BH1 one-fourth of the hip size 10 inches and from BH1, 1½ inches for looseness to BH2. Now set your center scale to the length of the back 43 from C to F, now deduct the finish above floor 7 inches, from F to L. Now measure from L to L1 one-fourth of the material required at hem, or 18 inches. Next set your side scale to the 43 inch mark for the side length, be sure the curve at top is on the curved line at B2, then get the length from B2 to L1 43 inches, less 7. Now connect L1 and BH2 with a straight line and draw a straight line from BH2 to B2 which completes the outline.

The seams with assembly notches must now be allowed and the hem shown, and for this lesson 4 inches will be allowed for a hem, the length of the hem is made according to the material used and the wishes of the designer, usually about 3 or 4 inches in wool or heavy materials and in silks, cotton or light materials they will be from 4 inches to 8 or 10, or in a great many cases, much more as in organdie, etc., where the hem is often the full depth of the skirt.

Ordinary seams should be ⅜ or ½ inch and in heavy goods or coats they should be ¾ of an inch or more.

Figure 3 shows the skirt pattern with seams and hem allowed.

To cut skirts for a prominent abdomen the curve at waist must be just reversed, that is, the front is cut curved up and the back curved down. See Figure 3, A1 and B2, which makes the front length the longest and back length the shortest.

To hang a skirt on the belt for a figure that is larger on one hip, raise the low side on the belt so as to cause the center front and center back line to hang straight, take in seam on small hip and let out seam on large hip.

Four-Panel Skirt

This is a modified gored skirt which means wedge shaped or pointed and is fitted closely to the waist and hips without the fullness used in the plain two-piece skirt.

The development is similar to that of the two-piece skirt except that there is no fullness allowed at waist and hip and the measurements around the figure are divided into four parts, as you can see on Plate 10, Figure 4, only one-half of pattern being necessary. The center front and center back alike (except for length) and the material for both would be cut on the fold. If it is desired the side panel may be cut in half on the center hip line H and HB and shaped from hip to waist as usual, which would make a six-panel skirt.

The broken lines show the development of the design as follows, see Figure 5, and make only one-half of the pattern from center front to center back. Place the three pieces together and start to lay out the design by making the distance from C to C1 three and one-half inches, from C1 to C2 two inches, then from C2 to the center back. Next decide how far below the waist you want the front of the yoke Y, this we will make 12 inches which will be 4 inches below the hip. Now locate Y1 7 inches below the waist and draw it as shown on Figure 4.

The distance from Y1 to Y is five inches so draw F1 one inch up from Y, this gives the center of the button and leaves 4 inches to be divided into the three folds F1, F2 and F3, which will make them one and one-third inches each. The belt is a straight piece cut three inches wide plus allowance for seams.

Always make the plain foundation first and develop the design on it. Then cut each piece apart and cut another piece for each and allow seams or other finsh.

Plaited Skirts, Figure 10

The word plait (or pleat, either is correct) means "to fold" and one of the methods used is shown on Plate No. 10, Figure 6.

For all fancy skirts, always lay out a plain foundation. A plain two-piece foundation is required for this one. Develop as follows:

Your pattern should appear just as the outline A and B in Figure 3. Now they should be pinned together with the side seams lapping from the hem to the hip, and above the hip to stand apart for the present. On the center front line of B, Figure 6, measure from W to H 8 inches, from W to L measure the net length of the skirt 42 inches less 7 inches which is 35 inches from W to L, measure from H to H1 4½ inches, from L to L1 6½ inches, then allow 1½ inches for the plait and one-half inch for seam H1 to H2, and the same from L1 to L2 2 inches. Now draw the line of the plait, the line H1 and L1 is where the plait folds under or back toward the center front. Now measure on the waist line from W to W1, 2½ inches and from the center front line to P, 2 inches. Now draw the curved line for the edge of the pocket first with a broken line until you get the desired shape and then draw it solid.

To develop the center piece or plait (C) take a piece of paper ten inches wide and the proper length 35 inches, then measure from the top or waist line down to H 8 inches and from H to HH draw a straight line all the way across the ten inches. Now measure from H to H3, 4¼ inches then 1½ inches more for the plait to H4, now from H3 to H5 measure 1½ inches more and one-half inch for seam, then from H4 to H6 measure 1½ inches and one-half inch for seam. Now extend all of these lines down to the bottom of the paper and cut out as shown on Figure 6 (C).

The back piece (D) is drafted just as you did the front (B), cut all three pieces out, don't forget to allow seams all around and a four-inch hem on the bottom.

The front piece (B) folds back on H1 and this line is placed on H3 and the seam at H2 and H5 stitches together. Then on the back piece (D) H9 folds back on the H8 line and this line is placed to H4, then H9 and H6 are stitched together.

You will notice that we have only considered the hip size and length. Now pin all three pieces together on the plait seams and pin the point P to the piece under it, being sure that both (B) and (C) are laying perfectly flat. Now follow the same instruction for (D) as you did for (B).

You will notice that the waist size is still 20 inches, which is half of the hip size, so lay little gathers or folds into the waist from W2 to W3 and from W4 to W5 until you get the desired size 13 inches which is half of the waist size.

It requires just three times the amount of material for a full plaited skirt as it does for a plain skirt and the reason is shown when you examine Plate No. 10, Figure 9.

You will see that the material is three thicknesses on a plaited surface.

Figure 9 shows a box plait in the center and side plaits on both sides, when this piece is turned over you have an inverted box plait with side plaits.

A sunburst plaiting is made by making the folds at one end of the material wider than at the other end, this causes the finished plaited piece to be fan shaped which is called a "Sunburst" plaiting.

The difference between accordian and knife plaiting is that the former is formed on a round edged plaiter and the latter is formed on a sharp edged plaiter; this makes the accordian plaiting more popular as it does not tend to splitting the material as much as does the knife or sharp plaiting.

This work is usually done by a machine made for the purpose, the material is placed in the hot plaiter then pressed together and when it is removed the plaits remain fixed.

Most of the large plaiting or kilting is done by hand in exclusive work and then should be done very carefully so that the edges will all be straight and parallel.

For a plaited skirt we always use the hip measure to work by; lay in the plaits to fit the hip then ease each one in gradually until we get the desired size for the waist.

All material to be plaited should be hemmed or otherwise finished before it is plaited.

Circular or Ripple Skirt

Tradition tells us that the circular skirt came into existence next after the fig leaf and the reason was that the ladies of those days took an animal skin, trimmed off the legs and head, cut a hole in the center of the back and draped it around her waist, allowing the fullness to ripple as it naturally would.

Be that as it may, we use the circular to a considerable extent today and probably will continue to use it in some form, if not with the full ripple.

Plate No. 10, Figure 7, shows the plain circular skirt.

The skirt machine will give the proper curves and measurements.

The full ripple skirt is cut so there is only one seam and it is down the center back and the curve for the waist as you notice is almost a true quarter circle flattened in the front. The less ripple in the skirt the straighter this curve becomes. For a skirt that is a full ripple or nearly so we do not attempt to fit the hips as it is not necessary or desirable. The full ripple skirt would probably contain 7½ yards around the hem on the medium sized figure.

The more popular ripple skirt for today is used for tunics, flounces, etc., and contain about 2, 2½ or 3 yards at the hem line; then if we cut this all in one piece we may dart the waist in above the hip in order to get a close fit just as shown on Plate No. 10, Figure 7 D, using either the one dart on either side, or the two darts, and in the event that we use the latter, we place them just as we do the seams in a four-panel skirt.

Place the machine on the edge of the paper as before, C and C1 (this design requires much larger paper), draw around the machine half of waist size 13 inches to W, measure down the center front as in the other skirts. Now measure from C to H the 8 inches for the hip and measure this 8 inches several places from the machine H1, H2 and H3. You will notice that the waist curves more as it goes toward the back, now measure half of the hip size 20 inches from H through H1, H2 to H3.

Now from L1 measure several places as at the hip and make the points L2, L3, L4 and L5. Now measure half of the material required at the hem; we will use 2 yards which will be 36 inches or 1 yard from L to L5; now draw a straight line from L5 to H3 and straight on to the waist, W1 (this must always be a straight line). Measure from H to H1 one-fourth of the hip 10 inches and measure from C to D1 one-fourth of the waist plus 1 inch, 7½ inches. Now measure from W to W1 and whatever this is, measure from D1 to D2, this gives the amount to take out for the dart D. The sides of the dart H1 to D1 and D2 must be shaped with a little curve by placing the 15-inch mark of your designing scale at the waist line D1 and D2. There must be a regular seam allowed all around and then a facing cut the exact shape of the bottom, as a hem must not be turned up on circular pieces as it would not lay flat, the facing for this is cut just as you have learned to cut other facings.

For a two-piece skirt with more ripple we must first determine just how much material is required at the hem, then cut the pattern just as you would for a plain two-piece skirt.

Skirt Variations

The light long broken lines on Figure 3, Plate 10, show the method for laying out scallops and other designs. The vertical lines running into the scallops show how to cut the sections apart and spread them in order to get a circular flounce by slashing the bottom and spreading the pieces apart (see Figure 8), then by cutting another pattern all in one piece you get a circular effect. Circular ruffling will be taken up later.

LESSON VIII

Plain One-Piece Dress

For this lesson paste two sheets of paper together so that it will be fifty inches long or longer; then place a pattern of your plain waist or blouse, made to the proper measurements on the edge, as shown by broken lines on Plate 11, Figure 1, make a plain two-piece skirt and add it to the bottom of the waist as shown on Figure 1. Now take another piece of paper and lay out the back in the same manner.

There is 1¾ yards of material at the hem in this dress, so the front must be 18¾ inches and the back 12¼ inches. The plain waist and plain skirt are shown by the broken lines. Now draw a straight line from the hem H and H1 to the armhole A and A1.

Proceed to develop the design as follows: The vest is four inches wide, which makes V to V1, 2 inches. It is cut 8 inches below the waist, so measure 8 inches and make the line LV to LV1.

The panel on the side is four inches from the vest line and it is 9 inches above the waist and 8 inches below the waist, so measure from P to P1, four inches, and draw the vertical line for the front of the panel PI, P2. The panel on the back is 3 inches from BP to BP1 and straight down to B2.

Now measure down from the normal or tight neck line V to the top the vest, which is three inches, and draw the top of the vest. Now make marks for assembly notches and cut apart.

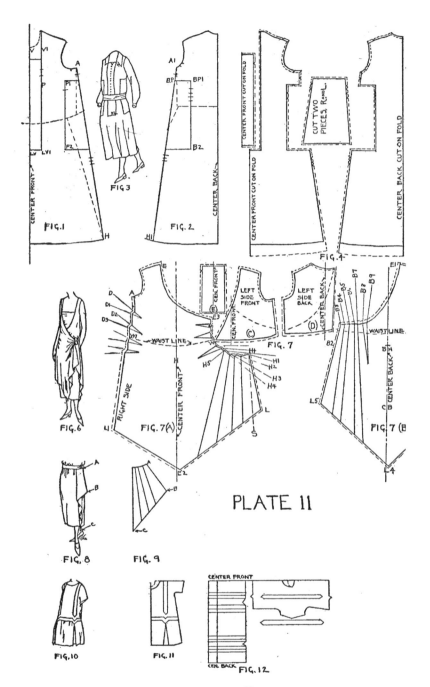

PLATE 11

32

Place the side panels together and cut all in one piece. The finished pattern should be just as Figure 4.

Don't fail to make the assembly notches, show all seams and mark each piece as shown.

The sleeve, Figure 5, is made just as you learned on Plate 7, Figure 3.

The cuff is a plain band 3 inches wide and 8 inches long with seams allowed which make the pattern 4 inches wide and 9 inches long; then it is folded through the center, making a narrow cuff 1½ inches wide finished.

The collar is made just as in Plate 6, Figure 6, except the end is shaped a little different.

Bear in mind at all times that all designs have a foundation and you have learned all of the foundations. The first thing to do when starting to make a design is to decide on the foundation, then make it and develop the lines therefrom.

The designs that are made on the Kimona foundation are developed the same as you did from Plate 11, Figure 1. The student must practice to get results and remember that "Practice makes perfect."

Draping

The easiest known method to drape a garment on the figure: First select the design, then study carefully every detail. When you have fully determined what foundation to use, whether princess lines, plain blouse, or kimona, then place material on cutting table and outline with chalk as much of the design as possible to cut by measurement, mark every point carefully, center of front, center of back (on each and every part), waist lines, back and front, shoulder points and seams and hip point; then, after stitch marking them so as to have them exactly the same on both sides, baste them together at all points possible; then place on form and drape balance carefully to the design that you have selected. You will find this will save endless hours of measuring and save one-third of the time usually required. If you have never draped before, then secure a soft piece of material about 4 yards in length and practice with this material until you acquire a soft drapy feeling in the ends of your fingers, that is, a feeling that by just lifting the material you can cause it to fall into any fold or line that you desire. The beginner must just drape and drape and drape until she has mastered the design selected. Trim away any surplus material and finish the edges according to the style. By raising or lowering the material on the figure or adding extra fullness in one place and stretching it at another, you will soon get in your finger tips the art of draping. We show you here the fundamental principles of draping, the outlines of the several different foundations, you could read hundreds of volumes and look upon thousands of pictures but you never can acquire the art of draping until you get it into the tips of your own fingers, and that is done only by practice. One design mastered means a good start on the road to a good draper.

Proceed to draft a pattern for the gown shown on Plate 11, Figure 6. You will see that both the front and back are cut surplice. Paste several pieces of paper together until you have a piece two yards long and at least one and a half yards wide. Then fold it through the center the long way and outline the surplice blouse as you learned from Plate 6, Figure 7. Be sure that the waist line is marked.

Now unfold the paper and measure down from the armhole at A 5 inches to D; then measure 1½ inches to D1 and fold this up in a drape and pin it.

Now measure from D1 to D2, 2½ inches, and from D2 to D3, another 1½ inches, and fold this up into a drape and pin it. Follow the same procedure with the other two drapes and make the finished length from A to LI, 29 inches. Pin each drape in the paper as soon as you fold it. For the drapes that go into the buckle on the left front, follow the same procedure as on the right side.

Now, at 4 inches below the waist line H measure out from the center front line H to H1, 20 inches, and lay off the cascade drapes from H1 to H2, 3 inches; from H2 to H3, 2½ inches; from H3 to H4, 2¼ inches; from H4 to H5, 2¾ inches. H2 folds onto H4 and H4 folds up to W. Now measure from H1 to L, 10 inches, placing L out about 3 inches from the straight line S.

Now get full length from point of shoulder E to point of Tunic L2, 50 inches. Now draw a straight line from L to L2 and from L1 to L2.

For the back of the tunic, Figure 7 (B), first draw your plain surplice foundation as you did for the front, with the paper folded through the center. Now unfold the paper and measure down from the waist line to BH, 4 inches; from BH to B1 measure one-fourth of the hip size or 10 inches plus at least one inch for looseness. For the drape on the back of the right hip measure from the waist line W3 to W4, 2 inches, and from W4 to W5, 1½ inches. Fold this drape up and pin it. Now measure from AI to L3 the same as the front, 29 inches.

Now measure from BH to B2, 18 inches; and from B2 to B3, up 7 inches; from B3 to B4, 2¼ inches; from B4 to B5, 2½ inches; from B5 to B6, 3 inches; from B6 to B7, 2 inches; from B7 to B8, 3 inches; and from B8 to B9, 1½ inches.

Now measure down from B3 to L5, 15 inches; and from CB to L5, 24 inches.

Now measure the full length of the back tunic from the shoulder E1 to L4, 49 inches.

Lay in the cascade drape here just as you did in the front.

The long curved broken line on Figure 7 (D) shows where you cut the surplice back from the tunic. This is used to draft the left side back of the bodice, which is made straight down to the waist line as shown.

The left front of the bodice, Figure 7 (C), is made just as you made the back, by using the piece cut from E to E3 as a pattern and extending it over the center front and down to the waistline as shown.

The vest, Figure 7 (E), is a plain piece, 10 inches wide and 13 inches long, attached to the lining.

The foundation skirt is made just a plain two-piece and the waist foundation is a regular French lining.

The student will no doubt have some difficulty in developing this design at first attempt, for it is one of the most difficult and most beautifully draped designs used in costume designing. She should practice over several times with the layout on paper and then develop the design in some soft material.

When this design is mastered there need be no fear of not mastering all of the rest.

The circular cascade, Figure 8, is cut similar to the one you just made, except that the top is cut circular just the size of the space it covers, which makes it perfectly smooth or without gathers.

Figure 9 shows the pattern for this plain circular cascade drape and the long, straight side stitches into the side seam of the skirt.

The student should practice these designs until she gets draping into the ends of her fingers.

Children's Dresses

A great many have trouble with designing children's garments. This is because they do not use measurements. Children's garments are cut on exactly the same principle as adults except that the measurements are different.

The student should take the measurements of some children that are at hand and practice cutting designs to their measurements.

The majority of children's garments are cut over the Kimona foundation as a little observation will show. Figure 10 shows a child's dress. Figure 11 shows the outline developed and Figure 12 shows the pattern. It is very plain that the principle is the same as for adults; therefore, the student should practice until she is familiar with children's measurements.

LESSON IX

Applique Cutting

The use of applique is popular more or less at all times and for many purposes; therefore, it is very necessary to have a quick method

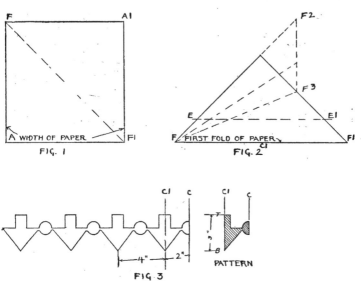

FIG. I

FIG. 2

FIG 3

PATTERN

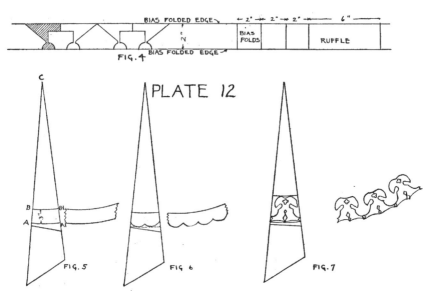

FIG.4

PLATE 12

FIG. 5

FIG 6

FIG. 7

for cutting it, which is given here. Applique is usually made from designs of fruits, leaves, points, scallops, squares or other geometrical figures and applied to the material with glue or fancy stitches. It should always be cut on the bias (or diagonal) or circular of the material. The material is folded so that a pattern for half of the design is needed; when it is unfolded you have the full design.

For practice work, take a square piece of paper, any size will do, the larger the better, Plate 12, Figure 1, and fold the corner A over to AI and you will have the same as Figure 2 F, F1 being the folded edge, which is the true bias.

We will select a simple arrow-point-and-ball design which will be four inches from point to point of the arrows, Figure 3.

The pattern must be half of the design or 2 inches from C to C1 and 3 inches from T to B. Now measure as on Figure 2 from F to E and from F1 to E1, 2 inches, and fold over and over on this line until you have a folded strip 2 inches wide, Figure 4. Now place the pattern of Figure 3 on the folded strip, Figure 4, and lay out and mark the design the full length of the strip and cut out the entire strip until the desired length of applique is obtained.

The student should start right in and cut out several designs from her own mind. In this way you will soon be able to make original designs.

Remember that the fold E, E1 to F, F1 on Figure 2, must be just half of the width of the design and the pattern must be for half of the design desired.

(Note that Figures 1 and 2, showing the paper, are drawn to a much smaller scale. Do not let this confuse you.)

Note Bias Folds and Rufflings, which require a great deal of time to make the old way, are cut in the same manner as applique by folding the material as you did for Figure 4 and measuring the width desired, being careful to keep your line straight across the folded edges, otherwise you will have crooked lines when cut apart. See Figure 4, Plate 12.

Circular Ruffling, Plain and Scalloped

Quite often great quantities of circular ruffling is required and cutting it inch by inch, the old way, is almost an endless job. Cutting straight pieces and shirring them up or cutting circular pieces by a pattern, one at a time, is extremely old style.

We will fold the paper and cut a plain circular ruffle. Fold your paper just as you did for the plain applique A to A1 in Figure 1. Now fold F1 on the right side over to F2, which gives you F3. Now fold F3 over to F2 line again and you have your paper folded as in Figure 5. Now start at the bottom and make a mark at A, Figure 5, and hold your tape at the point C. Then transfer the same length over to A1; this is to get a perfect circular.

Now measure from A to B and from A1 to B1, the width you wish the ruffle—in this lesson we make it three inches.

Now cut along the line A to A1 and B to B1 and you have a circular ruffle. Measure from B and B1 on up the fold and cut off pieces until you get the required amount of ruffling.

You can see that ruffling cut this way does not have to be shirred as it is already ruffled in cutting when applied to a straight line on the garment.

Figure 6 shows the way to cut circular ruffles with scallops; any design may be used instead of scallops. Fold the paper and lay out the plain ruffle just as you did for Figure 5, and then shape the scallop or other design and cut apart as you did for the plain scallop.

Full Circular Ruffling

Very often an extremely full circle is desired. This is obtained by marking the second fold on Figure 2 F to F1, then using C1 as the center or point, then cutting the ruffle as in Figure 5.

Embroidery, Braiding and Fancy Stitching Designs

Figure 7 shows the method for producing circular applique and embrodiery designs which can also be used for braiding outline and some very pleasing and original designs may be obtained in this manner.

Very often it is necessary to have a special original design for embroidery, braiding, etc. This is made just as you have learned to make the applique; ;then it is pinned on the material, stitched around the outline and embroidered in skeleton or filled in solid, or the outline is used as a guide for putting on braid, etc.

After the student has learned to execute this work on paper then she should practice with material, as this is where the time is saved. The lighter weight the material is, the more folds can be made at a time, and the heavier the material is, the fewer the folds, as it becomes too thick to cut with shears.

LESSON X

Discussion on Lines of Design

Contrary to the general belief that stout figures must wear harsh vertical lines, there are many designs that slenderize the more generously proportioned figures that do not have distinctive up and down lines.

Gracefully curved lines going around the figure with a circular fullness falling from them gives a stout figure of fair proportion a slender effect. For instance, a circular skirt or tunic sewed to the blouse at or slightly, say one or two inches, below the normal waist line will give a more slender effect than a straight gathered panel effect will do.

The main point in making designs for stout figures is to not fit the figure too closely, especially at the point where there is prominent fullness, for by fitting closely any curve that is not a graceful one you simply bring out the bad points when the object in view is to conceal them.

Every one knows a well proportioned figure of medium size can wear any design and it will be more or less becoming, but each and every woman has some individual points that can be made to stand out clearly by having clothes that are properly designed for her only. And this can only be done by studying the lines of each figure carefully until you acquire a working knowledge of the lines that are the most becoming to the different types, which is not difficult if you observe carefully the different people you meet every day and make a mental or written note of all the fine points that you see.

Materials of plain colors and neutral tones are better for stout figures. However, materials with irregular designs and medium stripes can be used and do not materially add to the size.

Never fit the waist line closely; a waist and tunic or a waist and skirt joined together and semi-loose will always give a slender effect. Long narrow vest front with flat neck finish or narrow semi-rolling collars are always good, as also is the surplus waist or dress. When fullness is added to the front of a garment at the shoulder, it is better to bring the shoulder seam forward, as this will make the shoulders seem smaller. (See Plate 6, Figures 3 and 4.) If plaits are used, then the shoulder seam should remain in normal position. If the hips are large, let the shoulders and hem of skirt be the main widths of a design. Never add any fullness that will give added width to the hips or waist. For a figure that is large in the shoulders and bust, use a short shoulder length, flat neck finish, V, U or square neck line with full tunic or skirt without defining the waist line.

For an extra large arm that is short, use a flowing sleeve with vertical lines and narrow cuff for hand finish. (The same rule applies to extra stout arms as to the body). By fitting it closely you add to the size. When an arm is short, do not use deep cuffs or several lines of division.

39

Glossary of Materials and Terms

This chapter gives a general description and definition of the most popular woolen, silk and cotton goods, laces and nets.

Woolen Fabrics

Woolen materials are made from the fleece of different animals, generally sheep. Quite often the wool is mixed with cotton or other material to lessen the cost of the fabric. A simple method to determine pure wool is to touch a thread to a match flame; if pure wool, it will curl up considerably before it starts to burn, and if there is a mixture the odor is easily detected as not pure wool, which has the odor of searing flash.

The following are the most popular and generally used woolen goods:

Beaver—Thick woolen cloth; weave similar to doeskin. The wrong side long thick nap.

Bedford Cord—Heavy ribs or cords running lengthwise in the fabric.

Botany Yarn—Australian wool used for worsted dress goods.

Bolivia—Similar to velours with uncut nap and glossy finish.

Broadcloth—Beautiful smooth pressed cloth; glossy finish.

Cashmere—Woolen cloth twilled on one side with a soft finish.

Camel's Hair—Loosely woven woolen; long hairy nap.

Challie—Very light woolen without twill; plain or figured.

Cheviot—Twilled nappy woolen cloth.

Chinchilla—Similar to Bolivia with uncut nap and dull finish.

Covert Cloth—Diagonally twilled cloth.

Esponge—Knotted thread loosely woven.

Homespun—With warp knotted to resemble hand-made thread.

Kasha Cloth—A camel's hair fabric.

Lansdowne—Silk and wool; very light weight; glossy finish.

Melton Cloth—Stout, smooth; the nap is sheared close to the surface without pressing or glossing.

Mohair, or Sicilian—Light weight, shiny, composed of wool from the Angora goat.

Poiret Twill—Fine diagonal twill or serge named for the famous French designer, Poiret.

Serge—Woven with a plain or twilled weave similar to a small cord.

Tricotine—Coarse diagonal twill.

Tweeds—Closely woven coarse thread fabric.

Velours—French for velvet, a pile fabric as plush.

Ziebline—Imitation fur cloth.

Silk Fabrics

Silk as we know it today is made by the silk worm, which is cultivated and raised especially for the purpose just as bees are raised to make honey.

The worms make the silk in cocoons or balls, from which the thread is spun which in turn is dyed or otherwise treated and woven into fabrics.

There is also on the market a cloth called Tussah silk, made from the silk of the wild silk worm.

In recent years chemists have perfected a process for using silky fiber from certain plants. This is known as vegetable silk and is used extensively in the manufacture of low priced materials.

There are hundreds of names applied to silks of various composition and manufacture. Following are the most popular and generally used silk fabrics:

Antique—Imitation of silks of former centuries.
Bengaline—Round corded weave of silk and wool.
Broadcloth Silk—Same as Pussy Willow with glossy finish.
Brocade—A silk woven with raised designs.
Canton Crepe—A crinkley rough surface crepe.
Chiffon—Transparent silk gause.
Crepe de Chene—Soft woven crepe.
Charmeuse—A very high grade supple satin.
Crepe Lisse—A thing silk gause.
Chiffonette—The flimsiest of the chiffon family.
Crepe Meteor—Fine woven crepe; satin faced.
China Silk—Thin plain silk.
Faille (file)—A soft ribbed silk running cross-wise, same as gros grain.
Foulard—A soft, washable dress silk, usually with figures of regular design. Twilled Foulard is really a silk serge.
Gros Grain—Ribbed with heavy cord running cross-wise.
Georgette—A heavy crepy chiffon.
Liberty Silk—Thin with a satin finish.
Malines—Very fine silk net.
Messaline—Light weight, lustrous surface.
Moire—A watered effect; used on all kinds of silks.
Pongee—Thin material woven from natural uncolored silk.
Matelasse—Woolen or silk cloth with a raised pattern as though quilted.
Poplin—A corded material of cotton, silk or wool.
Pussy Willow Silk—A heavy, firm, washable silk.
Radium—Brilliant or metal finish on silk.
Satin—Close texture overshot warp, rich glossy surface.
Surah—Light soft-twill silk.
Taffetas—A plain weave, hard smooth surface.
Tulle—Plain fine silk net of the chiffon family.
Tussah Silk—A rough surface similar to pongee, made from the silk of the wild silk worm.
Tricolet—Jersey silk weave similar to stockings.

Cotton Goods

Cotton, used so generally for thousands of purposes, is a vegetable which grows in warm climates. It develops a boll or ball, usually about two inches in diameter, which is filled with the cotton fibre and seeds. The seeds are ginned or taken out of the fibre, which is spun into thread from which the materials are made. The lint, or cotton dust, which comes from the fibre in ginning is used for padding, quilting and many other purposes.

Following are the most popular and generally used cotton fabrics:
Batiste—Fine cotton muslin; silky finish.
Bucram—Cotton cloth two or three thicknesses stiffened with glue.
Buther's Linen—A loosely woven linen, plain and smooth.
Cambric—Loose woven muslin, stiffened.
Calico—Printed muslin.
Cape Net or Rice Net—Stiff-finish Nottingham net.
Chambra—Similar to plain gingham.
Crinoline—Similar to cheese cloth, stiffened with a sizing.
Cheese Cloth—A loosely woven muslin without sizing.
Damask—With flat figures formed by contact between the warp and filling surfaces.

Dimity—White or printed; raised threads or cords running lengthwise.
Etamine—A coarse weave in cotton or silk; semi-transparent.
Gingham—A woven cotton material, plain or figured.
Japanese Crepe—A crinkly material made in Japan.
Mercerized—A chemical process for rendering cotton thread silky.
Muslin—Foundation weave from pure cotton thread.
Organdy—A thin, transparent muslin.
Percale—Cambric cloth closely woven, printed or plain.
Pique (Pekay)—Cotton cloth ribbed lengthwise.
Rep—Material ribbed crosswise, as cotton poplin.
Swiss—Hard, fine weave, usually with dots or St. Gaul designs.
Tarlton—Similar to crinoline, not so stiff in all colors.
Voile (French for veil)—Similar to Swiss, except it is a soft fine weave
    made in all colors and designs of cotton, silk or mercerized. De-
    signs are woven, printed or stenciled.

Laces

Lace material is woven in such a way that the arrangement of threads make the design. It is usually very open or porous. There are hundreds of methods of weaving it. The finest laces are woven by hand on a board filled with needles where the thread is woven in and out on the needle points, from which comes its name. Another method is to stretch the lengthwise threads (or warp) on a loom and work the design with a hand bobbin or shuttle, from which comes the name bobbin lace.

There are hundreds of different machines for making laces, embroideries, etc. One of the most popular machine-made laces is Valenciennes, commonly called "Val."

Following are some of the popular and generally used laces:
Alencon (Point d')—Fine needle-point lace.
Allover—Lace or embroidery where the design covers the entire sur-
    face
Antwerp—Bobbin lace, basket effect.
Baby Lace—Light, simple edgings made in England.
Battenburg—Hand-made of Battenburg braid.
Bobinet or Brussels—Plain net with six-sided mesh produced by
    twisting the thread.
Boubon—Machine-made lace of silk or cotton.
Brides—The slender threads that connect designs in lace.
Chantilly—Pillow lace very similar to blonde, made in both silk and
    cotton, usually black.
Cluny—Coarse thread bobbin lace, linen or cotton.
Filet—Square mesh net.
Flemish Point—Needle point lace made in Flanders.
Footing—Simple insertion of Brussels net.
Irish Crochet—A heavy white hand-made, distinctive pattern; very
    beautiful.
Irish Point—Applique embroidered on net.
Rose Point—Same as Venice.
Spanish Lace—Convent-made needle-point in large squares, or black
    silk in floral designs.
Point d' Esprait—A dotted net.
Torchon—Coarse open bobbin lace of simple pattern.
Venice (Venetian Point)—Needle point lace in floral pattern close to-
    gether connected by brides ornamented with picots.
Valenciennes—Bobbin lace, seen mostly in cheap insertions, common-
    ly called Val.
Van Dyke Points—Applied to laces with a border made in points.

General Terms

Applique—Designs cut out and applied to other material by stitching, embroidery or gluing.

Bias—Diagonal line across material.

Bayadare—Design that runs across material.

Brandenburg—Ornamental braid loop to use in the place of button-holes; commonly known as frogs.

Bouillonne—Narrow shirrings that edge wide ruffles of the same or other materials.

Caiman Cloth—Resembling alligator skin.

Chic (Shik)—Smart, good style.

Cloque—A line of straight embroidery ending in an arrowhead, used on hosiery.

Dresden—Applying to a very small, neat design.

Directoire—French style of dress of 1793 to 1901, reign of Louis XIV.

Empire—Style during the reign of Napoleon I; origin, Greece.

Fagoting—A criss-cross, open-work stitch done in rope silk.

Galloon—A narrow braid of gilt or silver on uniform.

Guimpe—A separate yoke and collar with or without sleeves.

Guipure—A coarse braid.

Incroyable—Same as Directoire. .

Linen—Thread made from the fibre of flax.

Lingerie (langeree)—Soft, dainty garments that may be laundered.

Maribou—Soft, down-like feathers.

Medici—A collar, high, stiffened, flaring out at the top.

Motif—The unit of any design. When used separately, it is called a medallion.

Nap—Right side finish on woolen materials that cut one way, nap running smooth toward the bottom of the garment.

Passementarie—Heavily embroidered edges and galloons of rich guampe braids, beads, silk, or tinsel.

Pile—Right side finish on velvets and plushes cut one way, pile running smooth toward the top of the garment.

Princess—Garment cut lengthwise all in one piece, fitted or semi-fitted, having seams from the center of shoulder, back and front, to hem, giving panel effect.

Rucheing—Narrow, plaited material stitched in the center.

Suade—Unfinished leather.

Picot—Small loop used as an edging on laces. ribbons. etc. Machine-made square holes stitched in garments, called hemstitching when cut apart; this makes picot edging.

Pinking—Edges cut with a pinking iron or machine to give fancy finish to seams, edges and quillings.

Warp—The lengthwise or longitudinal thread in a woven fabric.

Woof—The crosswise threads in a woven fabric.

Treatment of Colors and Shades

Many volumes have been written on the subject of color.. All of these works are available, but for the novice and inexperienced we give a much simpler method for acquiring a practical knowledge of the application of colors as applied to Costume Designing.

The student should supply herself with samples of material in all colors and shades of every description, which may be obtained from any dry goods store for the asking.

These should be tagged with the name of the material and the color that it is known by.

When wishing to select color combinations, first choose from the samples the body color or shade, then match the trimming shades with this sample until you get the desired effect. In this manner you will soon acquire the knowledge of what colors and shades harmonize or contrast.

For one who intends to make a serious study of colors a very important thing to do is to have a pencil and tab handy always. When you see a combination of colors or shades that are pleasing in a dress, hat or painting, write the combination down. This will also give you quite an assistance.

We reprint here a table of colors prepared by the Millinery Trade Review, of New York, an authority on millinery, which means color. This table gives contrasts and harmonies of the basic colors and shades.

REPRINTED BY PERMISSION OF THE MILLINERY TRADE REVIEW

Color Harmonies and Contrasts

The following table of color harmony and contrast is presented for the purpose of aiding designers and others who have to do with the planning of women's millinery, who are sometimes puzzled by inartistic results of trimmings that look well on one shade of a given color but that "scream" when applied to another tone of the same color. The reason may be found here:

White contrasts with blue and harmonizes with sky blue.
White contrasts with purple and harmonizes with rose.
White contrasts with puhple and harmonizes with buff.
White contrasts with brown and harmonizes with gray.
Cold greens contrast with crimson and harmonize with olive.
Cold green contrasts with purple and harmonize with citrine.
Cold greens contrast with white and harmonize with blues.
Cold greens contrast with pink and harmonize with brown.
Cold greens contrast with gold and harmonize with black.
Warm greens contrast with crimson and harmonize with yellows.
Warm greens contrast with maroon and harmonize with orange.
Warm greens contrast with purple and harmonize with citrine.
Warm greens contrast with red and harmonize with sky blue.
Warm greens contrast with pink and harmonize with gray.
Warm greens contrast with white and harmonize with white.
Warm greens contrast with black and harmonize with browns.
Warm greens contrast with lavender and harmonize with buff.
Greens contrast with colors containing red and harmonize with colors containing yellow or blue.
Orange contrasts with purple and harmonizes with yellow.
Orange contrasts with purple and harmonizes with red.
Orange contrasts with black and harmonizes with red.
Orange contrasts with olive and harmonizes with warm browns.
Orange contrasts with crimson and harmonizes with white.
Orange contrasts with gray and harmonizes with buff.
Orange requires blue, black, purple or dark colors for contrast, and warm colors for harmony.
Citrine contracts with purple and harmonizes with yellow
Citrine contracts with purple and harmonizes with yellow.
Citrine contracts with blue and harmonizes with orange.
Citrine contracts with black and harmonizes with white.
Citrine contracts with brown and harmonizes with green.
Citrine contracts with crimson and harmonizes with buff.

Russet contrasts with green and harmonizes with red.
Russet contrasts with black and harmonizes with yellow.
Russet contrasts with olive and harmonizes with orange.
Russet contrasts with gray and harmonizes with brown.
Olive contrasts with orange and harmonizes with green.
Olive contrasts with red and harmonizes with blue.
Olive contrasts with maroon and harmonizes with brown.
Gold contrasts with any dark color, but looks richer with purple, green,
Gold contracts with any dark color, but looks richer with purple, green,
blue, black and brown than with any other colors. It harmonizes with
all light colors, but least with yellow. The best harmony is with white.

Full Size Drawings

Full size drawings of all plates may be had by those desiring same.

Special plates showing development of new styles may be had when
Dame Fashion makes any extraordinary changs.

Free Students' Service Bureau

The Academy maintains for your convenience a Service Bureau for
purchasing materials or supplies and for furnishing any other information
desired, whether it pertain directly to Costume Designing or not.

On account of our ideal location we have at our disposal the best
Libraries and Museums on earth. which enable us to furnish almost any
information.

The stores of Washington carry complete full stocks of all materials
and supplies, both domestic and imported from which one may be supplied.

This service is free except for any special expense on account of the
individual.

This booklet is prepared for instruction on the use of Prof. Livingstone's French Dresscutting Machine. Information on any other instruction desired may be obtained through our Students' Service Bureau.

Machine for Sale and Instruction by Mail

The dresscutting machine with instruction book may be purchased out-
right. We also give individual personal instruction by mail, correcting each
lesson as it is finished and teaching the student where her errors are and
showing her how to correct them.

Examination Questions

After completing the course the student is given a general examination.

Diploma

Upon sucessfully completing examination graduates are awarded one
of our diplomas, for which there is made a nominal charge.

TABLE OF AVERAGE MEASUREMENTS
OF WOMEN'S FIGURES

WAIST

Front	14	14½	15	15	15½	15½	16	16½	17	17½
Underarm	9	9	9	9	9	9½	9½	10	10	10½
Bust	32	34	36	38	40	42	44	46	48	50
Chest	12	12½	13	13	14	14½	14½	15	15½	16
Waist	26	27	28	29	30	31	32	33	34	35
Shoulder to Dart	9½	9½	10	10½	10½	11	11	11½	12	13
Shoulder	5	5½	5½	6	6	6½	6½	6½	7	7
Neck	12	12½	13	13½	14	14½	14½	14½	15	15½
Back	16	16	16	16	16	15½	15½	15	15	15

SLEEVE

Upper Muscle	9½	10	11	12	12½	13	13½	14	14½	15
Shoulder to Elbow	14	14	13½	13	13	13	13	13	13	13
Elbow to Hand	10½	10½	10½	10	10	10	9½	9½	9	9
Hand	6½	7	7½	8	8	8	8½	9	9½	9½
Lower Muscle	10	10½	11	11	11	11½	12	13	14	15
Inside Length	20	19½	18½	18	18	18	17½	17½	17	17

SKIRT

Waist	26	27	28	29	30	31	32	33	34	35
Hip	36	38	40	42	44	46	48	50	52	54
Front	40	40	40	42	42	42	43	43	44	44
Right Side	41	41	41	43	43	43	44	44½	45	45½
Left Side	41	41	41	43	43	43	44	44½	45	45½
Back	41	41	41	43	43	43	44	44½	45	45½

This table was compiled from averages of actual measurements taken for custom-made patterns.

BV - #0035 - 200922 - C0 - 229/152/3 - PB - 9780243089598 - Gloss Lamination